For the family Barbara, to remember their grandmother June Nordquist and Auntie Fern
Love from Leda

Silence on the Bridge

SILENCE
on the
BRIDGE

Leda Stegel Darlington

ACKNOWLEDGMENTS

My thanks to Christina Dubois for the help, encouragement, and moral support she provided in bringing this second edition to life. I also appreciate the support of my grandchildren—Chase, Chloe, Chelsea, and Clara—and my sister and brother-in-law, Wilma and Leo Niosi, and their son Jeffrey—my everyday comforter with a cup of coffee.

SILENCE ON THE BRIDGE

ISBN: 978-1-72400-368-3
Second edition, 2018, printed in the United States of America

Published by Leda Stegel Darlington
Editor: Christina Dubois
Designer: Christina Dubois
Printer: Kindle Direct Publishing

DEDICATION

THIS BOOK IS dedicated to everyone who has contributed to it, one way or another, especially:

My husband Ed, who encouraged me in this project and faithfully helped me along the way.

My husband's mother, Beatrice Tilliard Darlington, an extraordinary woman who raised her children with very little help in Butte, Montana, during the Depression. She was an inspiration to me.

My mother, Yolanda Soltesz Stegel, a brave woman whose sole purpose was the welfare of her family. She knew deep inside she was not going to escape the tragedies and sorrows that fate had in store for her. She saw the future and tried to change it for the best, only to eventually lose everything precious to her. She could foresee the future—she was a true psychic—but she felt her own predictions were working against her and she could not change the forces of destiny, just like in the opera, La Forza del Destino. She believed that life was already written and, even with trying, we could not dramatically change its course.

My father, Philip Stegel, the optimist, who remained hopeful throughout his life, despite our family's losses. Even in the worst of times he could always ask: "What can be done?" and then proceed with the task. He always found a way. He believed in a happier future and held to the conviction that each person makes their own life. He told me many times: "Don't be upset, just laugh. Life is too short." His saying was, "La vita comincia domani (Life begins tomorrow)," while my mother's was, "La vita é un sogno sfuggente (Life is a fleeting dream)." They wrote these sayings in my memory book before I left for the United States.

This book is a gift to my children and their children to help them understand their heritage.

CONTENTS

PREFACE

ONE OF MY ambitions has been to write a book. I first had this thought many years ago when I was taking courses in English for my nursing degree. Growing up here and there, I never had a continuous education that was not interrupted by some event. In nursing school I was finally getting a real education. My first goal was to have a profession. I worked as a waitress to pay for my college education and finally became a registered nurse in 1975. Not only was my profession rewarding, it gave me independence.

My second goal was to write about my experiences in a clear, interesting, and informative way. It is amazing how far back one can remember. I can see scenes and episodes from when I was three, four, or five years old. I wanted to write a book that speaks about my family as far back as I remember.

It would almost appear as if I came from nowhere. I can account only for my sister, Wilma, who lives near me in Tacoma, Washington, although I know of some cousins and their descendants living in the United States and in Europe.

My life has not always been happy, and for this reason I could not start writing. I was afraid to be sad again. This fear held me back for several years, but that changed when I took a creative writing class. I found that I could write meaningful episodes that were fun to read, and so I overcame my fear of writing about the past. Lebanese-American writer and artist Kahlil Gibran wrote, "Where there is sadness, look deeper, and there is joy." The sadness was not there anymore, and I did not find myself crying all the time. Instead, I found joy in remembering all the significant people in my life.

I came to the United States in 1950 when I was fifteen years old. I came with my sister, two years younger than me; we were refugee children of postwar Europe. The war devastated our family. In a supremely unselfish act, our parents decided to let us emigrate, hoping for a better life for us. In their distressed situation, they could only envision a life with little chance for an education or job training if we stayed in Italy. A short time before coming to the United States, I worked in the office of the company where my father had been employed. No doubt people were trying to help us while my father was unable to work, but at age fifteen I lacked the skills needed to earn a paycheck.

Neither of our parents was in good health, either physically or mentally. They were distressed by the death of two sons and by a life that was becoming more difficult with the loss of earnings that resulted from my father's illness. He had contracted tuberculosis while spending the war years in a forced-labor concentration camp in Germany.

After the processing of much paperwork, my sister and I arrived in Bremerton, Washington. We lived with two sisters, June and Winifred—both high school teachers—who came to live together after June's husband died.

Whenever I speak, people ask me where I am from—this after over sixty years of living in this country. I am from Italy originally, but America is now my home. It is of little consequence where one is from. What makes a person is one's experiences and how one responds to them—people, events, and places that have touched one's life. Accents are just interesting speech patterns that have nothing to do with what a person is saying.

Life is a fleeting dream. I feel I have to catch this dream before it ends and memory fades. I have to leave a written account of my family. It seems long ago that my mother was trying to tell me of her youth and her life. I was too young, and then she was gone before I was able to understand. My mind was always on such matters as what to wear to school the next day, assignments not finished, anxiety over catching the little train to school early in the morning. But somehow I must have heard, because now I remember, and I can see how remarkable my mother and father were.

On one of my latest trips to Italy I visited the city where I was born. Most of all I wanted to see where my brother was killed, the little village of Buie, not far from my hometown of Fiume. It brought back memories of traveling with my mother to the farms in that area, bartering for food. In those hills there were a lot of partisans (resistance movement forces) and Germans fighting during the war.

Life goes on; there is joy and sadness and also the future. I have so much to be thankful for: my sons—always good babies, toddlers, teenagers, and adults—and their father, who always believed in me. My greatest wish is for all four of our boys, my sister's and mine, to be good friends and share each other's life experiences; to help each other as they did with their paper routes, in snow and sickness, and be there for each other always.

INTRODUCTION

THERE IS SOMETHING very intriguing, even spiritual, about a bridge. It can form a connection between two important places and for this reason might be an enemy's first target. Sometimes it is referred to as a place for leaving this world and entering another. Sometimes it is a special meeting place.

The bridge on the cover of this book is of special importance to me. It is from a picture that was taken in 1938, close to the time of the events you will soon read about here. It divided two cities: Fiume, then in Italy, and Sušak, then in Yugoslavia (now combined and part of Croatia). The little river beneath it was really just a creek coming from the mountains and draining into the Gulf of Quarnero near a port able to hold 150 large ships. The bridge was low, with barely an incline from the piazza on the Fiume side. The stone arch under the bridge was typical of many in Italy.

Long ago, an old stone bridge stood in its place, probably constructed by the Romans, who built summer residences to the south, along the Dalmatian Coast. Diocletian was the emperor who built an entire city there in Split. No doubt the Romans regularly passed through Fiume to get there.

In my life, this particular bridge brought both good and bad tidings. I will never forget the day in 1945 when the bridge brought deafening silence. I vividly remember my mother holding me, saying nothing. We waited for hours, until it was very dark. There was nothing but silence on the bridge, and we were all alone.

I was ten years old.

1 THE WAR

WORLD WAR II began when I was four years old. I remember hearing the cries of the older children, "The war started! The war started!" as they ran up and down the streets, screaming as if to let everyone know. Of course, it was all over the radio stations, but the children were excited and thought they were providing a valuable public service. I don't know what was going on in their heads, but I wasn't too thrilled. Too many times I had seen serious men in our house, talking about what they heard on the radio. Their discussions sounded fearful and worried.

My father's coworkers and friends often gathered at our house to discuss politics. Our house was a busy place sometimes in the evenings, and noisy too. At times I would go in my parents' bedroom and stare for a long time at the picture above the head of their bed, and I would feel at peace. That picture had been there for as long as I could remember: the Madonna kneeling beside her child in his bed, and the baby peacefully sleeping.

I studied the features of the mother of Jesus; she had an anxious look and tears in her eyes. This picture gave me a sense of comfort and, at the same time, some concern. Why was she crying? Did she know already of the fate of her son? I loved that picture so very much, and it was a comfort during the long evenings of political discussion in the kitchen when I could not sleep.

When the air raids began, the sirens became a familiar sound, but they never failed to awaken a deep fear inside me. Most of the time I could hear the airplane bombers approaching long before the wail of the sirens began. When I heard the muffled roar of the airplanes in the distance, my legs would become weak. My mother was always surprised

Map showing the boundaries of Italy prior to World War II.
Courtesy Gigillo83, Wikimedia Commons

when I told her the airplanes were coming because she could not hear them. Nobody else could hear them as I did.

Sometimes the sirens would sound four or five times a day. Each time everyone would run to the underground shelter that served our neighborhood. My brother Ireneo would carry my sister, Wilma, on his shoulders and pull me by the hand. Sometimes he even tried to carry me in his arms while Wilma clung to his neck. Mother would limp behind us. Father would be in one of the shelters at the shipbuilding foundry where he worked.

There were many such shelters throughout the city, each typically an underground cave. The natural terrain of the whole area is solid rock, filled with natural tunnels and caverns. The caverns were prepared like the rounded mines of the ore prospectors in the hills of Idaho, as I have seen them on raft trips. This region around Fiume is called Carso. Not far from there is the famous Grotte di Postumia (Postumia Caves) in Slovenia. Looking at a map today, I have difficulty finding the villages or towns I knew because the familiar names have been changed and are now in Croatian. For example, a nearby vacation city, Abbazia, is now Opatija. The little town of Buie is now Buje, Pola is Pula, and Postumia is now Postojna. My world was only Fiume—now Rijeka.

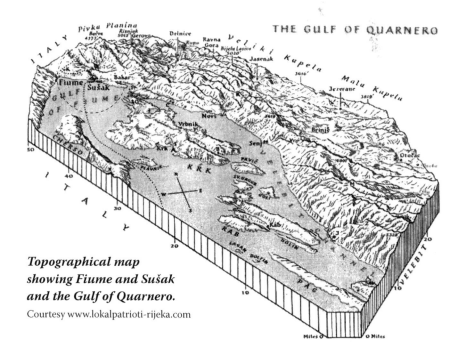

Topographical map showing Fiume and Sušak and the Gulf of Quarnero.
Courtesy www.lokalpatrioti-rijeka.com

2 THE PICTURE

THE PICTURE IS of my family when I was very small. I am certain my mother's sister, Irene, was the photographer. She was the only one in the family who owned a camera, and she loved taking photos. It is because of her that we have some pictures of our past. To visit us, Aunt Irene had to travel most of a day on a train from Milan (Milano), where she lived and worked, to where we lived in Fiume, on the other side of northern Italy.

In the photo, my father and mother stand proudly in front of our house with my two brothers, Ireneo, fourteen, and Sergio, ten. My sister, Wilma, in my mother's arms, is about one year old. Ireneo is holding me, and I am about three. It is the most wonderful and warm picture. I can see the love of my dear aunt who posed us all and then returned to her spot to snap the picture. As she was unmarried and had no family of her own, she would cherish this photo until her next visit.

This may have been the last happy picture of our family, taken as it was before the war—before our house was bombed—and we with no idea of what was to come.

The camera my aunt used was an old-fashioned Kodak with accordion bellows. She would hold it at waist level and look down into the viewer. The old camera showed everything upside down, as in a way everything soon would be when our world, as we knew it, would vanish.

I remember well the scarf and the heavy, warm beige coat I was wearing. Many of our clothes came from Milano or were made by my mother. My sister wore a homemade knitted coat, blue and red, with no buttons—only two strings to draw it together. My brothers wore the

The Stegel's family, about 1939. Front: Leda; middle: Ireneo and Sergio; back: Papa, Mama, and Wilma.

regular heavy wool attire of that era. My father was in his best jacket and my mother wore her best dress.

3 Home in Fiume

MY EARLY CHILDHOOD is the most wonderful part of my memory. It is amazing to me that I would remember so much from age four or five or even younger. I realize now how much children can assimilate and retain for the rest of their lives.

I have noticed that children with a good wholesome childhood become very happy adults. Children need to grow up in a nurturing home; they deserve it. The first few years belong to the child, to enjoy and learn about the world. My mother said of neglected children, "They didn't ask to come into the world." Now that the parents have the children, they are responsible for them, was her attitude. She was very worried about children being neglected. I heard her say, "*Questa bambina é ben portata su* (This girl is well brought up)," of a child she approved.

I don't remember being scolded or disciplined. I only remember wonderful times of playing with dolls or other toys that my brother made for us. We were taught manners and respect early, and there wasn't anything to be scolded for. We knew what was expected. Our life was much simpler than it is for children today. Our toys and activities were stored on shelves we made ourselves. We'd gather weeds and grains or seeds, berries, and small rocks; some sizes of rocks represented potatoes. Then other children would come and buy these imagined valuables with pretend money.

There were other homemade or invented games, like playing theater. We acted little plays on a made-up stage, dressing up with Mother's clothes, Father's tools, and anything we could find. We would take turns being actors and spectators.

The setting of my hometown was similar to my present hometown of Tacoma, Washington. Fiume, of course, is much older than Tacoma.

This ancient city is situated on what was then the border between Yugoslavia and Italy, but it is now part of Croatia. The city has an important working port, just like Tacoma.

Fiume was built by the Romans. In antiquity the city was erected on a hill named Tersatto; in fact, it was originally called Tersatica, built in defense of the valley between the mountains and the sea. Although from 1860 to 1918 Fiume was under the control of the Austro-Hungarian Empire, it had an autonomous government and had never been part of the Slavic group of countries—Croatia, Slovenia, Serbia, and so on.

During World War I, Fiume was under Austro-Hungarian rule. Afterward it became part of Italy. I was born in Fiume in 1935, when it was part of Italy and all the inhabitants spoke Italian. However, because it was a border city, people also spoke Slovenian, Croatian, German, and other languages. There were many Hungarians there as well. Of course, children went to Italian schools, and no other language was offered.

Because the city had always been autonomous, it remained under its modern name of Fiume, the Italian word for river, until after World War II. It was then that Fiume came directly under Yugoslavian rule, and its name was changed to Rijeka. When Croatia left the Yugoslav federation to become an independent state in 1991, Fiume/Rijeka went with it.

My father's family was Slovenian. He was born in Fiume and was an Italian citizen. My mother's family was from Hungary. She never considered herself Italian, and she never spoke perfect Italian. In some of her sentences, words were out of sequence, but her pronunciation was excellent.

Fiume's central core, called Citta Vecchia (Old Town) was the original city where many families, most of them poor, had lived for generations. They had dwellings that were passed down to the next in line in the family.

I thought Citta Vecchia was an interesting place when I was small, but it was not a place we would go very often, and never without our parents. It was easy to lose track of children in the narrow streets. Mothers then as today were fearful of their children being stolen. My mother had a strong hold on our hands if we went there.

Buildings were only two, three, or four stories high, set among narrow and hilly cobblestone streets. It was like a maze, and a child could be easily lost. Laundry crossed over the streets, hung high on ropes and pulleys. The streets were lined with little places to eat and shops selling bread, meat, and vegetables. Each little store specialized in one item, such as meat of a different cut or a store with varieties of breads. There was also an open-air market where farmers brought in their goods.

People lived in apartments above the shops and went into the streets to buy and barter every day for fresh goods. It was very noisy in every little street, either with music or crowds of people talking loudly. There were little arguments at every corner, or so it seemed to me, with crescendos of voices in open, loud discussions. Citta Vecchia was not for children, and I went there only a few times with my mother.

To get to downtown Fiume we had to take a long ride on a streetcar. The center of the city was several miles from where we lived. The railroad line was below the hillside, running along the waterfront and the shipyard. The busy port area was in the city proper. From the hill above the city we could see the big stacks of ships at the docks and continuous traffic in the bay, with big and small boats.

This bustling area, not far from Citta Vecchia, was the heart of the city. It was crowded with the people of Fiume, foreign sailors, as well as Italians. Near the port square was an impressive church of Gothic architecture. It was faced with red stucco and had a bilateral-tiered staircase up to the entrance. It is still a landmark featured in postcards.

Fiume is surrounded by hillsides sprawling with houses and apartments of the working middle class. We lived in a corner apartment on the bottom floor of a *caseggiato*, a two-story apartment building, containing ten units. We had a neighbor above us and another alongside, followed by a row of others. We never heard the family upstairs from us, and we didn't know them very well. Next door to us lived a professor and his wife and daughter, whom we rarely saw.

Leda, Sergio, and Ireneo (left to right), in front of Mama, holding Wilma, and Papa, about 1939.

The happiest part of my childhood took place in this home on Via F. Redi (Francesco Redi was a seventeenth-century physician and poet). Our family was all together and we had relatives who lived close by, so we could visit. Although it was always a dream of our parents to have their own house, it was not as common in Fiume as it is in the United States. I remember going with them to the very outskirts of Fiume, far from where we lived, to look at a small lot in the middle of nowhere. They talked quietly of building a house on this lot while I stood nearby. It never happened, but we sometimes went to look at the place.

We could have used a lot of space around us. With four children, our family was large compared to the rest of our relatives. There were only a few families with many children—usually Fascists trying to please Il Duce (Benito Mussolini). Most of my aunts and uncles had one or two children or none (in 2001, Italy had zero population growth). I believe Mussolini was giving money for any child born at that time. My parents never applied for such a thing, of course.

Our home was immaculate; mother could often be seen meticulously cleaning and treating the different floors with polish. Our apartment had three bedrooms, a kitchen, and a bath. The front entrance had an enclosed porch where we left our shoes—they were never to touch the polished floors.

After this porch was a hallway lined with bedrooms, the bathroom, and a storage room. The kitchen stood at the end of the hallway. The hall and kitchen had marble floors while the bedrooms had parquet floors. Marble and tile floors are very common in Italy. There was a large bedroom for our parents and two smaller bedrooms—one for my two brothers, and one for my sister and me.

At the entrance were many *pattini* (skates) or pads my mother made of thick material, usually from old wool coats. She stitched several layers of material together into inch-thick pads to fit our feet. Leaving our shoes on the covered porch, and we stepped into our "skates" and slid around on the polished floors, which we thought was great fun. All the children who visited our home had to do the same thing. In the summer we went barefoot outside.

The kitchen was the place in our home where everything happened. When I was three or four years old, time seemed to stand still and life was happy. My father worked at the shipyard foundry. In his spare time he would build and maintain rabbit cages and shelters for the chickens and goats. Mother would have dinner ready as soon as my father came in. She would instruct us to remain quiet and good because "Papa is tired."

Mother was an extraordinary cook, and everything she made tasted simply special. When we were growing up, even during the war, we had a nutritious diet, mostly from our garden and animals. We had a vegetable garden plus chickens, rabbits, and goats. My mother's sole purpose was to take care of her family in the best way possible, with good food and a pleasant, clean house.

I don't remember eating sweets until I was about ten years old when the American soldiers gave us candy and gum. Candy was certainly not a daily addition to our meals, as it often is in American families. On holidays we had homemade desserts such as strudel and *oresniaza* or *potiza*, dialect words for a type of pastry made with nuts.

My two older brothers would help with the chores while my sister and I played. There were rabbit cages to clean out and animals to feed and water. They would gather all the animals for the night into their respective shelters—herd chickens up the stairs to their roost and take the goats into their sheds.

My Aunt Irene would come to visit a few times a year. She brought us many good things we otherwise would never see: dolls, toys, little undies, and shirts. We thought she was glamorous because she dressed in stylish clothes and lived in the big city of Milan during our childhood years. I knew that, though my mother was now a housewife who wore simple, handmade clothes, she had been like that, too, in her youth. I had seen pictures of her beautifully dressed in the style of the day.

All too soon the war would break out and our happiness would be shattered, replaced by a seemingly endless stream of tragedies and losses.

4 THE SIMPLE LIFE

OUR LIVES CENTERED around home and family activities. Father had to milk the goats. He knew so much more about farming than my mother. I always sensed that my mother was having to adjust to this kind of life. In her younger years she had been a well-dressed *commessa* (shop clerk). Father could do everything, even butchering—a job he did not like. When it came time to do this, he became silent and thoughtful and did not want anybody around. In an area behind the stalls he skinned the rabbits and spread their fur on boards. He had studied how to do the tanning in a book. I remember many furs ready to use, but I never had a coat made of fur. I think my mother simply did not know how to go about it.

My parents worked together for the good of the family to prepare for the cold winters and absence of fresh vegetables. Some winters were very long and cold, with the bora and rain that kept us from going out of the house. A bora is a north-northeasterly downslope wind in the Adriatic Sea that could easily pick up children even when they were holding onto ropes in the streets.

My father learned many farming skills from his own mother. She was from a family in Monte Nero (Crni Vrh), Slovenia, where traditions were passed on, similar to the American pioneers who canned everything. When I visited this area later in life, the old houses were still intact and their large gardens were thriving with vegetables. I could imagine how my father and grandmother did the same sort of things, working together, preserving food for the winter.

Ours was a colorful neighborhood, but I believed then that we were different from all the other families. We were the only ones, for instance, with animals and a large vegetable garden. Even so, each family seemed to have different customs. Altogether, this made us a rare breed of people, which were truly Fiumani. In Trieste, they were truly Triestini, with common traits such as being quicker in speech and action. Mother said, "*Vera Triestina*," by which she meant quick and shrewd.

Papa watering the flowers.

The family that lived next door—a professor and his wife and daughter, Ornella—was completely isolated, or so it seemed to me. Ornella was a little older than I. Maybe once I saw her father, and I never saw her mother. Their garden, in contrast to ours, was all flowers, with an empress tree near the alley dividing our house and garden. Under this tree all our animals were housed in the little sheds my father built.

The garden was enclosed with a wire fence; wood fences were never seen in Italy. Across the alley, our home had a little cement walk that went around to the front door. Between the walk and the house was a flower border filled with geraniums, asters, zinnias, and roses that made a colorful sight. Special herbs grew everywhere and were much used. Father would often make sage tea, reputed to be good for colds, chest congestion, and sore throat.

We had so much—a nice home, a big garden, and many animals. Every spring there were new goats, baby chicks and rabbits, and a variety of hens. It was exciting when my father would come in early in the morning and announce the arrival of two new kids. We'd run to see them, barely able to stand up on their wobbly legs.

I can still recall my father teaching Mother how to prune roses, speaking in a soft voice. He was very patient and tolerant of her ignorance. His childhood had been so different, with his own mother teaching him gardening and canning, and the two of them working together at the family business after his father died. He had a special ambition to raise many different kinds of chickens and other animals. We had leghorns for eggs and the red chickens for meat. There were white-and-black speckled hens and bantams. It was fun to have different species and colors of chickens. We also had ducks and geese that roamed free in a little courtyard fenced off from the vegetable garden. We had long-eared Angora rabbits in brown, white, and black. Mother never did utilize the Angora wool. She just didn't know how to remove it from the rabbits.

The goats were the most fun and the most intelligent. They had to be taken to pasture wherever there was grass and edible brush. We had nothing for goats in our garden; the leftover vegetables were given to the rabbits. Both animals loved hard, old bread.

Sometimes I was assigned to take the goats to pasture, and other times it fell to Sergio. I would hold onto the rope tied to their harnesses

The four children, with Papa in the background.

while they moved about, feeding on the hillside around Fiume. I loved this job, and I loved being out in the fields, but sometimes it was a little lonely. I kept the thick rope close, following them as they pulled the rope and watching them eat and make their little contented "behh, behh" sound.

I loved the smell of the earth, the countryside with its patches of dry grass. I would sit on a rock and look around the hills and little valleys. In the summer it could be very dry, but the goats managed to find leafy pastures. The air could be hot, but there was always a breeze coming up from the Adriatic. I didn't find it boring; it was a job somebody had to do.

Earlier I had tagged along with Sergio, but as we became bigger and older, the harder jobs went to the two older brothers, and soft jobs like pasturing fell to me. My sister, two years younger, did not have any jobs yet. I knew that Pippi and Sergio would do any job assigned to them and more. We were all "working for the family." There was no more important goal than this, except school, of course.

The goat milk tasted very strong, and I never liked it, but it was fine used in cooking. My father usually milked the goats. I always felt that my father could do anything in the world.

Father and Mother worked together to make sauerkraut in barrels. I watched my father teach my mother this process. He would start with one layer of thinly sliced cabbage, then salt, then more layers of cabbage and salt, in an orderly fashion to keep it flat. Finally, when this process was done, he would cover the top of the crock with a fine net and a heavy wooden lid that he had made for the purpose. On the lid he would place a heavy stone to press the cabbage down. Turnips were preserved the same way. What was left of any vegetables would be taken to the rabbits. There was no such thing as pellets or prepared food for them.

I have such warm memories of Fiume. Living in Florence after the war that fragmented my childhood, I longed to return to my native city and the wonderful life I had known there. But that life had vanished like a dream.

5 OUR NEIGHBORHOOD

BESIDES OUR BEAUTIFUL home, we had a large, wonderful garden. The chicken coops were built off the ground and had little steps for the birds to climb in and out. Every night their doors and windows would be shut, and the chickens would perch on the pole across the top of the coup. In the morning my father would let them out before going to work. Later, my mother would feed them and collect the eggs. The goat sheds were large enough for my sister and me to use as playhouses when the goats were outside. My father cleaned them often; he liked the animals to be in clean sheds. My sister and I could pluck pods from the tall pea vines and eat the young sweet peas. Sometimes we would pull carrots and bright red radishes from the ground.

An interesting family lived across the courtyard from us. There were eight or nine children, which was an unusually large number for that time and place. The oldest girl, Aurelia, who was about eighteen, would come often to visit my mother. She was always coughing, and she was so thin and stoop-shouldered that when she coughed you could see her bones outlined under her light cotton dress.

My mother would fix fresh eggs for her or zabaglione. To make the creamy sweet pudding, she would break two eggs into a bowl, then blend with sugar using a spoon as an eggbeater. She also fixed other healthy foods for Aurelia. While doing this, she would keep my sister and me busy so we weren't underfoot while she and Aurelia were visiting. Mother was very tender and warm to the girl as they visited. They spent good times together. After Aurelia went home, I would see Mother with tears of worry in her eyes. I knew she felt helpless and unable to do more. Aurelia's family destiny of too many children and too little income was playing itself out, and even my mother could not intervene.

Eventually I learned that this girl, neglected by her family, had advanced tuberculosis. Her father was often drunk when he came home, and her mother was always busy with a new baby. Their house was run-down, and at dusk I saw cockroaches coming out of it. Their home was infested with the bugs and had a very old, bad odor, unlike the clean smell we were accustomed to in our house. I could smell that odor from the street outside.

I felt very sad for all those children; they did not look happy. They always played by themselves—the other kids in the neighborhood stayed away. I made a big effort to remember their names, but today I can only think of Aurelia, a fragile girl with long brown hair and deep, sad eyes.

With four children, our own family was considered large, but the family across from us passed all reasonable limits. There was another family in the complex that had many children, but they all looked well-fed. I heard some people say about Aurelia's family, "They want to please Mussolini and get extra money for each new baby!" One time I heard my mother say of Aurelia's father, "Oh! Oh! He is coming home drunk again! Another baby will be on the way."

I loved my neighborhood and was happy there. But then the war started, and we had to run to the shelters when airplanes flew overhead. A few times I saw the bombs shining in the air, whistling as they came down. My older brother Ireneo would try to reassure us, saying they were not aimed at us or our houses. After a bombing, I would hear him and my parents discussing it. They said if areas near homes were hit, it was only a mistake, a target misjudgment. My father said it is difficult to judge and aim just right. Their talk had an air of forgiveness and acceptance, rather than blame.

It was not very pleasant in the shelters, so we would run home after the curfew. Many times, we had to run back to the shelter again shortly after getting home because of another air raid. Ireneo carried my little sister on his shoulders and pulled me along. I was scared and shaky until we got to the shelter entrance under the sheer rock face. Then we descended gradually into the long corridors underground.

It was like going into a mine, only these tunnels did not need roof support because they were carved in solid rock and were also made larger and taller. These tunnels would go right through, across the mountain, opening to the other side of the hill. There were two entrances. Here we were safe from the bombs, but it was very disturbing when there was an explosion close enough so my ears would feel the rush of air through the tunnel. I would cover my ears as soon as I could, but they still hurt.

It was important to find a good location in the crowded space of the tunnel where we could spread out blankets and set up folding chairs. We had to stay there several hours sometimes, until the sirens would signal the end of the attack. My mother would not let us stay there any longer than required because, with so many people crowded together, she felt the shelter was too damp and unhealthy. Often we didn't get there fast enough to get a good place, so we had to sit on the damp floor.

Sometimes when the sirens would sound, my mother would not be able to keep up with us during our run to the entrance. She had been injured as a small girl in Budapest and had a difficult time with her left leg, which was fused at the knee. We would wait at the shelter entrance and were so relieved when we saw her come limping in. Sometimes she would not be there, and I would become very apprehensive. After Sergio's death I was afraid she didn't care enough to run from danger. When the curfew was over I would run home; only after seeing her could I breathe normally and quiet my anxiety. I remained very fearful for my mother, and I always stayed close by her. Later I would not let her go anywhere alone.

6 SPECIAL HOLIDAYS

IN THE WINTER months, when the days become short and dark, small children stay inside the house, safe and warm. At this time of year in Fiume and Trieste there often comes a bora—a strong, cold, northerly wind that is almost like a little tornado. The sound of the wind is alarming and eerie.

One winter event we prepared for was Christmas. For this we would scrounge all over the hills and woods for the special *muschio* (moss) used for the *presepio*, which is a miniature nativity scene. We gathered all the *muschio* we could find, then at home we would prepare a table for the scene. We carefully placed all the moss to resemble the hills where Jesus lived long ago. Then we placed little figurines, the manger, the animals—sheep, donkeys, and camels—and the one or two shepherd figures we had. This nativity scene was in every house. I am sure nobody had a Christmas tree, because I never saw one.

This family holiday was very peaceful and happy. Mother would make many sweet cakes, cookies, and always the rolled-up walnut pastry that was typical for this season. We called it *oresniaza*, which I'm sure is a dialect word only used in that part of Italy. It was not easy to make; I helped with mincing the walnuts very fine. It is done similarly to strudel, which is made with apples. Mother made both of these pastries, and many cookies.

Our family was a little different because we were not Catholic, but this was still a special time for us. Other Italians have many more holidays, especially with their patron saints. Our parents were Protestant. They even gave us names that did not have a patron saint: Ireneo, Sergio, Leda, Wilma. As different as we were, I never wished to be Catholic, with all the rituals and the ornate churches. Our Waldensian church was very simple, with only benches and a pulpit—no saints on the walls and no statues. Our pastor had a black tunic, which he only wore during the service. Afterward he would be in regular clothes, talking quietly to all the churchgoers. It was an atmosphere of respect and friendship—very supportive, quiet, and peaceful. I loved going to our church.

New Year's Eve was another event for us. We went out armed with pot lids and at midnight would start to bang the lids together, making a lot of noise. There was noise all over because everybody was doing the same thing. I knew that this was to bring in the New Year and be happy.

Children also know that on a certain day in January, a very old woman in a long black dress will be roaming the streets, bent over her cane. Mothers admonish children to be good. My mother would say, "If you will be good you will get some toys. If you are bad you will only get a sack of coal." Mother, a stranger from another country, followed all the Italian customs with her children.

On that night I would peek from the window to see if I could spy La Befana, the old woman. One time I thought I did see her, before I ran to hide. She was all bent over, with toys sticking out of a bag on one shoulder. On the other shoulder she had a smaller sack, all black. It was exciting, and we could hardly go to sleep that night.

The next morning I went outside to look for the gift from La Befana. She was always good to us, and we never found any coal. La Befana was indeed a very good grandmother, and I knew she loved children.

Our cheer and fun ended before I was six years old. These happy occasions became only a memory after the start of World War II.

7 WORLD WAR I

ALL THE QUALIFIED men of the region had to enlist in the Austro-Hungarian army. The region included eastern Italy, Slovenia, and Fiume, where my mother's brother, Paolo Soltesz, and my father, Philip Stegel (Lippi, as he was called), lived as young men. An old picture shows the two of them together. They were comrades during World War I and visited each other's homes after the war.

My father grew up in Slovenia and later Fiume, in a close-knit family of very religious people. As a child he was an altar boy in the family's Catholic church. The children in my father's family worked with their mother to do all the chores: taking care of the horses and other animals, preserving food for the winter, and even making slivovitz (plum brandy) with the abundance of plums in their lot. The many relations on both sides of the Stegel-Premeru family often held festivities together where the men were sure to have a glass of the potent drink.

Philip was popular as a young man. He had a good voice and was agile in the local traditional dances. He could lead the party in wonderful evenings of native Slovenian songs and opera arias. His eldest sister, Zinka, was proud of him when he became the man of the family after their father's death. She had in mind a number of young girls she deemed acceptable for him to marry.

In contrast, Uncle Paolo grew up a stranger in the country he came to live in after his family emigrated from Hungary. His mother could never speak the language of his contemporaries. Their large family was not well-to-do, and tragedy befell at least two of the children. They had only one another and no other relations. After the death of their father, all the children able to work had to do so.

My father's family was not happy when he became good friends with Paolo's sisters and brother. Eventually Paolo's sister Yolanda (my mother) charmed Philip, and they were married. She was not from what Aunt Zinka considered a desirable family, and, worst of all, she was not Catholic.

For a few years, Zinka was the real head of the family. She was smart and skillful but also opinionated, and she had no tolerance for "infidels," as she called anyone who was not Catholic. She was a strong influence in the family. Growing up, I was not aware of any of this, except for a child's extra perception. I sensed that my father's sister felt she had little in common with us.

While Nonna (Grandmother) Stegel visited us for several days off and on from Split, about 160 miles southeast of Fiume on the Adriatic Sea, Zia Zinka came to the border with Nada and Zivko, her own children, only for a very short visit at the iron gate. Either she did not have the stamp to enter Italy or did not wish to visit us at our home. Later in life, when I was here in the United States, we all became very good friends. We wrote many letters back and forth, finally getting to know one another.

My father's mother was all the family we needed and wanted. Nonna Stegel, who could speak perfect Italian and, most of all, our familiar dialect, was very different from Nonna Soltesz (my maternal grandmother). Nona Stegel loved us so much. She played with us and was a perfect grandmother. Her expression told me she loved to be with us. Her hair in a bun, white as snow, and her roundish figure under her black skirts invited lots of hugs, and she hugged back with sweet kisses on our cheeks. She made up for everything.

8 ORNELLA

OUR GARDEN WAS a magical world for me. I loved and was in awe of the big empress tree, at least thirty feet high. It had large, tropical leaves. Although now I know this tree is deciduous, I don't recall ever seeing it bare. It was truly majestic. In the spring it became completely covered with exotic purple flowers. It dominated the corner of the garden where the goat, chicken, and rabbit houses were situated.

A little farther over, there was the open area of the vegetable garden. It flourished with tall bean stalks, peas, and all the low vegetables, such as lettuce and green peppers. The root vegetables were also divided into sections of beets, potatoes, radishes, and turnips.

I remember two neighboring families who made an impression on my five-year-old mind. The two-story brick apartment complex where we lived had another just like it on the other side of a little courtyard. We were at one end on the bottom floor of the first complex. One neighbor lived across the courtyard and up one story; this was a big family. Part of the bargain for living on the bottom floor was that we could have a piece of land. I am sure when our family first moved there, we chose this corner apartment for that reason. I am also sure there was nothing but rubble or a wild area where our garden now flourished. No doubt, Father transformed it.

The other neighbor family I remember was adjacent to us, with their garden alongside ours. This was a very small family. Their garden was an enchanted place for me. It did not have vegetables but was like a tropical jungle that we could barely see through. The fragrance of roses and other flowers drifted into our yard from that isolated world. It was very quiet there and even scary at times. I never heard any sounds, only the rustling of leaves and bushes. I could never see anyone there but could hear some motion and sense a presence, like one feels a ghost.

Sometimes, I sensed the presence of a girl of about six or seven in the garden and caught a glimpse of her apron. I knew this family had a little girl, and I knew her name was Ornella. She was already going to school while I was still too young for school. She was the only child of these reclusive neighbors. I never saw them outside, and the father must have left early in the morning for work. Their entrance was hidden from

*Leda and Wilma in the family
garden, about 1940.*

our house. Their porch, like ours, was enclosed completely with vines of wisteria (*glicini*).

I would try to spy through the branches, but I could not see through the trees and thick vegetation. I wanted to talk to Ornella, but even when

25

I made a sound she would not answer. She must not have had permission to talk to us. This little family was very private and isolated.

Our own family was not one to mix with the others in the complex. My parents were just too busy and kept to themselves. But we had a lot of coming and going between house and garden. I don't think my mother even knew the names of the other people living in the complex. She had nicknames for different people. There was *la grassa* (the fat one), and *gambe di spaghetti* (legs of spaghetti); the Germans were *gnocchi* (potato dumpling) because they were thick-headed. The worst was *testa di capuzo*, for someone not too bright.

One day, all life disappeared from the magical garden. After several days I realized that the house and garden had been abandoned. The family was gone. The garden was silent—no more little footsteps.

The mystery was never solved for me. For a long time I went near the garden to listen, but I could not hear the hesitant little steps on the leaves, trying to hide their presence. I could not hear someone brushing against the bushes or have the unmistakable feeling of a presence there even though I could not see it.

Something must have happened, and I felt sad and even lonely, as if I had lost a friend. For a long time I could see the ghost of a girl walking through her garden, I could smell the fragrances drifting with a little breeze, as if the rose bushes were being touched by a little girl's hand, but all life had gone forever.

That was the start of the war years. German soldiers were marching all over town as if to impress everyone with their power. They seemed to be everywhere, looking for all kinds of people to take as "prisoners of war." They would come in small little platoons of four or six, or even twos, but it seemed to me they always marched. They did not walk normally, in a relaxed manner. They had very noisy boots that clicked on the sidewalks. Most people were unaware at this point of what was going on and I only had a child's instinct. I dreaded seeing German soldiers, and I was afraid of them.

They had rifles across their shoulders, handguns at their waists, and belts of bullets. The German soldiers always looked taller than other people—even my father, who was at least six feet tall. Their impressive uniforms and all the guns and boots made them seem so much bigger. Even our Italian *bersaglieri* (sharpshooters) or *Alpini* (a mountain warfare military unit) were not as imposing.

The garden remained silent and was no longer fun—only very sad.

9   THE GOOD LIFE

WHEN ONE IS born into a nurturing family that values the needs of the children above anything else, one is very rich. Ours was such a family. As far back as I remember, my father worked long hours in the shipyard. After he came home he would work in the vegetable garden and care for the animals. My mother had our meals on the table at a regular hour, and these meals were wonderful and nutritious.

Only a mother's cooking can be like that. Mama used the vegetables from our garden, and for meat we had chicken and rabbit. The goats were kept for milk only. I am certain I never ate goat meat. My parents were not farmers, but they believed in self-sufficiency. A single paycheck was not enough for a family of six that included four growing children, even in those days.

These are memories of my preschool years before the war started. Mother kept the house immaculate: we each had our own bed and children's furniture. My parents' bedroom had a beautiful mahogany set. Mother valued her furniture. I saw her polishing the wood with special oils. It always looked like new, with not a scratch or blemish. In Italy houses came completely empty—no closets, shelves, or cabinets. All furniture was paid for at "a rate," that is, monthly payments. Mother insisted on a better style of living than the other families around us.

The master bedroom consisted of a mahogany bed, an armoire, a dresser and mirror, and chairs. The children's bedrooms contained lesser quality, plain furniture; for us girls, it was white wood. Likewise, the kitchen furniture was all white—cabinets, marble-top table, and wooden chairs. As I have said, we were never allowed to walk into the house wearing shoes. I would often see Mother on her hands and knees, washing the marble floors and polishing the parquet floors in the bedrooms.

My father built shelves in the bathroom and in our small indoor storage room. This may not be a talent possessed by many men in Italy, even today. When I visited in later years, I found that people were inclined to call an *operaio* (craftsman) to repair or build something. However, my two cousins in northern Italy, Ezio and Franco, are very handy "do-it-yourself" types who make their own repairs.

My brother Ireneo was already an apprentice in the shipyard, while Sergio was always bringing home things that were useful in one way or another. My sister Wilma and I were cared for and loved by our brothers, who were always protecting us and talking to us like two little men. They never interfered with our games and friends. I don't remember any of us fighting or being disagreeable with each other; the job of reprimanding was for our parents. We all had some jobs to do, and one of mine was collecting eggs sometimes with my mother.

Almost all our aunts and uncles lived in Fiume, except for Zia Irene and my father's sisters. When Aunt Irene came to visit us, there was a holiday atmosphere. She always stayed with our family because she was so close to my mother. We would be excited for days before her arrival, and there was a constant question: "When is auntie coming?" Zia Irene was so much younger than my mother that she was more in tune with us kids.

All this happy life ended with the death of Sergio, and then the war. Our beloved Sergietto was gone and our happy life was gone . . . forever, it seemed.

10 HAPPY CHILDHOOD,
THEN A FADING DREAM

OUR KITCHEN WAS a gathering place. Here we all ate together, our family with four children, while my mother served Hungarian food. She preferred to cook Hungarian dishes instead of Italian. She was a very patriotic Hungarian in every way. She never spoke perfect Italian—she transposed some words and had her own particular syntax. I only knew she did not talk with the same accent as other Italians. This fact made her even more singularly special to me.

The kitchen was a meeting place for my father's friends and co-workers. At these times, without being told, we children knew not to come in and out of the kitchen. The kitchen door was closed and serious discussion of politics was going on. All the men had their say, and my father was one of the leaders for the "cause." I always listened with my "third ear"; I could often hear Father's strong voice, talking about *giustizia sociale* (social justice). I was tuned in, even while playing out in the hall. We did not have a radio in our house, but I had seen people putting their ears to a radio in other homes, listening for the news. And now these men were discussing what they heard on the radio.

My mother served them *palacinche*, a sort of crêpe suzette, and wine. She never had to come out to admonish us about being loud or disturbing. We children knew what was expected, and I don't remember my mother ever scolding us or having to explain. Actually, they were a lot louder in the kitchen now and then, their voices rising to a crescendo, then diminishing to a single voice.

The talk was about eminent war, all the injustices, the Fascist regime, and the Germans. It sounded disturbing, and I was apprehensive when these meetings took place. I had seen the Germans in their impressive uniforms, in big groups marching in the streets, their boots making a roar in my ears. The Fascists were also marching a lot, wearing their round caps with the bouncing tassel and their shiny black knee boots.

A group of little girls was playing in the hallway: my sister, me, and two other four-year-olds. The hall was close to the kitchen. We were playing quietly, probably because we wanted to listen in. My brother Ireneo was often with them, mostly listening. My brother Sergio was usually outside, busy with his wanderings around the neighborhood or countryside.

I remember playing games during my childhood, as kids in other countries do: a group of little girls holding hands and going around and around, singing:

Giro giro tondo.
Casca il mondo.
Casca la terra.
Tutti giù per terra.

Turn, turn around.
The world is falling down.
The earth is falling down.
Everybody's sitting down.

And we would all fall down. When we were outside in bigger groups, we would hold hands to form a large circle, then play the singing game that went, "*O quanti figli avete, madama dorè?* (O how many children do you have, Madama Dorè?)" One half of the group would answer and step inside the circle. This game had definite steps and it was for older girls; I was not usually included and would just watch.

There was also a performing time where the bravest of girls would sing a song in front of the other children. There were special songs that everybody knew, like *"Mamma"* and *"La via del bosco (The Path in the Woods)"* and so many more that I now remember only when I hear them. Luciano Pavarotti has sung many of these old songs.

My Aunt Irene, for whom my brother Ireneo was named, would come and visit a few times a year from Milano. She had a very simple

Wilma and Leda, about 1939.

job and very little money, but she always brought gifts, bought with her small savings just for us. Mostly they were gifts of clothes, but one time she brought beautiful dolls for my sister and me. I would clutch this doll in my arms so tightly that nobody could take it away from me.

We would not have had any of these nice things if it weren't for Aunt Irene. My sister and I were the little daughters she never had. My mother was in her forties when my sister and I were born. She had many worries and not much patience. She was worried about my seventeen-year-old brother because he was nearing the age when he would be subject to the military draft. Aunt Irene was a big support to my mother; the two sisters were very close.

Many thoughts were going through my mother's mind. Joining the Fascist army was not really a choice for my brother. Our family was never pro-Duce, even though the whole country followed Mussolini. Other kids in the neighborhood joined the Fascist youth groups: *balilla* and *figli della lupa* (Sons of the She-Wolf). We were not part of it. Sometimes I was jealous, thinking, "Why can't I also wear these pretty uniforms and go to special marching events?" Before the war it seemed as though everybody was a Fascist; after the war it appeared that nobody wanted to admit this openly.

There was a feeling of uneasiness, and after meetings at our house, even the usual accordion music did not lighten up the men's faces. Somebody in the group always brought an accordion to play after a while and include the children in the fun and songs. In every crowd in Italy there was always someone who could play, and all would join in to sing the old songs.

Even then, I had a feeling that life as I had known it was coming to an end. Children are so well-tuned to their surroundings. Yes, I knew our beautiful life was coming to an end, but the first tragedy that hit our family had nothing to do with the war.

11 MY BROTHER SERGIO

I WAS PRESCHOOL age, but I remember my brother Sergio well. He was ten years old in 1940 and had blue eyes and sun-streaked blond hair. He was lean but strong and athletic, with an outgoing, truly giving temperament. He was always ready for any chores or requests from our mother.

Sergio could always make my mother smile, with a little joke or a tease. Her face was serious most of the time, but I could see her smile when Sergio talked to her, even laugh at times. He was a consolation to her; he understood her worries and made light of any subject he could, even bugs that he would capture. He was also a great storyteller—tall stories, of course. The two had a special relationship, as if he was making every moment precious for her. Was it because there wouldn't be very many more? It is strange how some people sense so much before it actually happens.

Sergio would never come home empty-handed from his excursions. It might be just a few apples or a handful of nails, or even some pieces of wood that looked good to him. All these things would come home for some future use.

My father kept the tools and supplies he worked with very organized. He had a little cubicle on the porch where he kept all his tools, nails, and screws. He always had the right tool for the job, and I remember he valued every little tool, whether it was a hole punch or a drill. Whatever Sergio brought home was appreciated and stored in neat order for possible future use: big nails in one box, screws in another, all according to size. The tools were usually hanging on the wall.

One day in late summer Sergio was gone on his usual adventurous trips around the countryside. He was always very busy roaming about

Sergio, 1940.

with friends or alone when he was not needed at home. Usually I did not pay attention to him as I played with dolls, dressing them and rearranging doll furniture.

Then one dark day came when our world collapsed. It was September 1940. I was only five years old, but I remember vividly all the details of that day.

12 THE BOOTS

EVERYTHING WAS FINE for Mother until she saw his boots. She had been waiting for him, worried about him, and now she finally saw him coming home.

He was average in size for his age, his intelligence showing in all his features. He had a perfectly shaped boy's head, and his facial expression showed alertness and passion. He loved his life, his family, and his adventures. I remember him in Tirolean-style short pants and a white shirt. His arms and legs were browned by the sun at the end of summer.

He was my brother.

This day Sergio had gone on one of his usual adventurous trips around the countryside; he could travel well with his worn-out boots. On this particular day, he came home with his hands full of ripe figs to give to Mother. He would never come home empty-handed. He always had treasures to bring his family, either some trinkets for his little sisters or something he thought would be useful for my father or mother.

He went past me, limping. His cheeks, always bronzed and flushed with excitement, were now pale. His sun-bleached eyebrows wore a frown, and his blue eyes were troubled with anxiety. He went to mother and I ran behind him. After looking closely, mother saw that his worn-out ankle boots had streaks of dried blood and his left knee was covered in dirt mixed with blood. He had a deep wound on his knee.

He told Mother, "I wanted to get some ripe figs to bring home."

"Where was this?" Mother interrupted.

"A long way from here. I have been walking home for an hour or more, but the knee really hurts and I could not walk faster."

So Sergio had walked, limping, while his wound bled. Seeing him with his knee bleeding frightened me. He was in pain—I could see it in his face—but he did not complain or cry. I had a deep feeling of sad omen; anxiety was churning in my stomach. The fragrances of late summer, of mixed flowers and ripe pears and apples permeated the air. These were the fragrances of our safe home, but they did not comfort me.

Mother called out to my fourteen-year-old brother, Ireneo: "*Presto* (right away), go get Papa at work." He was working at the *cantieri navali*, the shipyards, just below our house. She was visibly shaken by this accident but tried not to show her concern, so as not to alarm me as I was watched the whole scene intently.

Sergio continued his story. "The fruit was high up in the tree. I climbed up, then the branch broke, and I fell on some rocks under the tree. There were mules and cows tied to the tree." The area had droppings from the animals.

My father came quickly, as the foundry where he worked was just below our house, which overlooked the port on the outskirts of the city. Ireneo and my father clasped hands with their arms crossed to form a portable chair for Sergio. After Mother lifted Sergio on the make-do sitting gurney, they started for the hospital, which required taking a little train to get into the city. Mother followed them. I waited at home for Sergio to come back from the hospital.

When he returned the next day, Mother settled him in a chair on the porch, propping his legs on another chair. Something had changed about him. He was quiet, drawing pictures with colored pencils. He kept busy and did not talk much. Every day my mother brought him out on the porch, cool with the surrounding wisteria. He created wonderful art for Mother. The drawings revealed beautiful gardens with a myriad of flowers and blue skies. He was peaceful and serene now, not in pain, and not anxious to go somewhere to explore. He was calm and so good to me, calling me to see the drawings, asking, "Do you like them?"

One last drawing I remember was of a cemetery with many white crosses; in the distance, crosses were vanishing, giving way to the bluest sky. Beyond, the scene opened to a beautiful land of trees, flowers, and bright light. I could not help exclaiming, "*Il paradiso* (Paradise)!" I realized later that Sergio was preparing Mother for the trip he would soon take to a world of incomparable beauty.

"Three days—that's all we had with him," cried my mother later. Then the dark day came when they had to take Sergio to the hospital again. The doctors admonished my mother to let him go in peace. They did not let her see him in the last throes of tetanus. All attempts to save him were in vain, and Sergio died within a few days. I heard Mother and others saying often: "*In pace* (In peace)." They had to let him in go in peace.

Our family was now lost without the enthusiasm and love of Sergio. When my mother lost Sergio, she also lost a big part of herself. The child who had brought so much love and understanding was gone. After his death, my mother was never the same. Black clothes were all she would wear from then on.

Sergio knew that he was dying, and during the few days at home he prepared my mother as best as he could. The pictures of bright light and ethereal countryside were for her. At the last he told her not to worry: he was going to be in such beautiful places and he would be happy in the hillsides of trees and flowers.

I remember my dear brother in a child *bara* (coffin), all dressed in white—a beautiful, sleeping angel. Tears would not stop flowing from my eyes, and I was walking around like a shadow, not talking at all, hiding in corners, hiding from the world that had collapsed around me.

13 THE LETTER

IT FELL TO Ireneo to inform the family on my father's side of what had happened. My mother's family were all in Fiume, but Father's mother and two sisters were in Split, Croatia. Here is the letter in Italian, written as a boy of fourteen, with some dialect words and problem punctuation, followed by an English translation:

Fiume, 23 X 1940

Mia carissima Zia Zinka,

Con immenso dolore Ti annunciamo la morte del nostro Caro Sergio. Che e avvenuta il 25 di Settembre alle ten di sera.

La mamma e papa' sono tanto addolorati che non possono scrivere neanche alla nonna, perche hanno paura che Le fara male.

Per questo Ti scrivo a Te; il 16 Settembre il giorno fatale, Sergio e cascato da un albero di fico, ha fatto una ferita sotto il ginocchio; papa' lo ha portato subito all'ospedale dove gli hanno fatto tre punti; otto giorni stava bene, ed in una volta il male si aggravo' e subentro il tetano, venne portato con l'aubulanza all'ospedale di nuovo, dove, dopo due giorni e due notti con atroci sofferenze moriva. Gli furono fatto il funerale che riusci assai bello.

Intervennero molti bambini e ragazzi, suoi amici colle famiglie, il coro dei ragazzi hanno cantata il Miserere, e molti conoscenti fra i quali anche la signora Prade e tanti vostri conoscenti. La Nonna Soltesz tanto piange e non si puo consolare, e giusto ieri e andata ad abitare da zio Paolo perche qui tutto Le ricorda Sergio che gli voleva tanto bene.

Io Ti ho scritto tutto quello che sapevo, un giorno si decidera forse anche papa' a scrivere meglio alla Nonna.

Sergio e un angioletto che pregara per noi tutti; qui Ti aggiungo una copia del culto che il nostro Pastore ha tenuto al cimitero.

Saluto in nome di tutti noi, voi tutti.
Boris

Here is the English translation:

Fiume, 23 October 1940

My Dearest Zia Zinka,

With immense pain we inform you of the death of our dear Sergio, which happened on 25 September at ten in the evening.

Mama and Papa are so sad and in such pain they cannot write, not even to Nonna, because they are afraid she will suffer and become ill.

For this reason, I write to you. The 16th of September was the fatal day. Sergio fell from a fig tree and suffered a wound under the knee. Papa took him right away to the hospital, where they applied three stitches.

For eight days he was well, and then suddenly he became very ill, and his condition worsened and tetanus developed. He was taken again to the hospital with the ambulance, where after two days and two nights, with atrocious suffering, he died. On the 27th of September there was a funeral, which was beautiful.

There were many children and boys, his friends, with their families. There was a chorus of boys that sang the Miserere. *There were many, many friends, among them Signora Prade and other of your friends.*

Nonna Soltesz cries so much, and she cannot console herself. Just yesterday she went to live with Zio Paolo (she lived with our family a few years) because here everything reminds her of Sergio, whom she loved so much.

I have written you everything that I know. Maybe someday Papa will decide to write a little better to Nonna (Stegel, his mother).

Sergio is a little angel who will pray for all of us. Here I attach a copy of the service that our pastor had at the cemetery.

I send greeting to you in the name of all of us,
Boris (as he was called by Father's side of the family)

14 THE LOSS

MY MOTHER NEVER seemed to recover after the loss of Sergio. It was such a tragic death and so sudden. He was only ill for a few days after the accident. The wound was taken care of in the hospital, but when tetanus attacked his system, we were helpless to do anything.

My mother kept an enlarged photograph of Sergio on her bedroom dresser. Her eyes were dark and deep set, and she was always crying secretly. As I accompanied her on her daily shopping errands through the streets, I saw her studying boys the same age as Sergio. She was in some way in denial of his death.

I remember well an incident that revealed she could not console herself. One day she came home with a boy who actually looked like Sergio. I studied this boy and his features, staring at his expressions and his manners. The resemblance was very close, but I knew he could not be Sergio. Sergio had love pouring out of his being; this boy was harsher in his manner.

Mother had found this boy playing in the streets and asked his parents if he could spend some time with our family. I had a feeling that his parents happily approved of this arrangement. He was not from a well-to-do family, or even a family like ours. He did not have good manners.

I don't remember the boy's name, but I know my mother kept trying to see Sergio in him. He stayed with us a few days, but it soon became apparent that he was nothing like the innocent Sergio who was full of love for everyone and tender with animals and even insects. Wise in the ways of the world, this boy was not kind to our animals nor to us girls. He deceived my mother, acting one way with her and then taking advantage of her depressed condition. He even stole.

After a short time he was gone. Either he left, which I believe really happened, or my mother took him back to his home. He was gone as suddenly as he had come.

After this short uplift, my mother was once again plunged into deep despair. She was always quiet and sad. At one point I discovered that, after putting us to bed, she would walk to the cemetery in the dark and spend a good part of the night at Sergio's grave. When winter came, I was worried and afraid that she would be found frozen on the tomb. Winter in Fiume can be very cold, with a strong wind—the bora. A few times I walked to the cemetery, fighting my own fear, and convinced her to return home.

Then the war started, and more sadness was soon to come our way.

15 THE BOMBING

THE AIR RAIDS started and shelters were made ready for us deep in the mountainous region where we lived. The distance from our house to the shelter was maybe three blocks. After the entrance there was the moderately steep descent into the tunnel, into the deep rock of the hillside. As we walked farther inside, the path would become darker and darker until there was light only from our lanterns.

The tunnel enlarged about halfway down, into a natural cavern. Here was the biggest concentration of people. Some would always either reach the shelter early or reserve their space. They'd stake out their spot, even taking turns in keeping it for their family or friends. Most people preferred the spots nearer the entrance since the air became very stuffy farther in.

We usually had to walk far into the cavern to find a place to sit. Most people brought folding chairs and blankets, and for the most part just sat and waited. Some people would lie down and cover their ears. When the bombing would start, compression waves would go through the tunnel. This was a very uncomfortable feeling, especially in the ears.

Sometimes we had to stay there for three or four hours, but eventually the sirens would signal the end of the bombing and we could go home. Sometimes there were curfews that lasted the whole day because the bombers would came back many times at short intervals.

The shelters were damp and cold, so we had to wrap ourselves in blankets for long periods, just waiting for the signal to come out. Occasionally the sirens sounded too late, especially after we had just emerged from the shelter and returned to our homes. At these times I would see the shiny, silver bombs dropping with a whistle all the way down from the airplanes. They were aimed at the ships in the harbor, maybe.

We were reassured by Pippi (Ireneo) that the bombs would not hit our home. From the attitude of my family, I had a feeling that these airplanes were really our friends. As a child I was able to assimilate what was going on around me; I don't remember a lot of explaining by our parents. Discussions of the war were not shared with children.

Most of the city's homes, including ours, were on the hill overlooking the water and were generally out of danger. But one day we came back from the shelter and were shocked to find that one of the bombs had landed in our yard. There was a big hole in the ground and the huge, majestic empress tree was lying on its side.

The vegetable garden was totally destroyed and the animal pens flattened. Our goats, rabbits, chickens, and ducks were all dead. Our house was like the mouth of a cave. Almost all our beautiful furniture was smashed, and all the windows were broken. We had to dig through the rubble to salvage clothes and any other belongings we could find. Only one cabinet and the Singer sewing machine were nearly intact, spared by a thick wall.

All the fruits of our family's labor had been destroyed in an instant.

16 MY FATHER'S YOUTH

MY FATHER WAS the oldest of four children—two brothers and two sisters. His father, whom I knew only as Nonno (Grandfather) Stegel, was long gone when I was small, but I learned some important facts about him from my father. One year he suffered a stroke; a few years later he suffered a second one, which he did not survive. He was still fairly young, most likely in his forties, when the first stroke left him paralyzed on his left side. His left arm was useless, and he was unable to use his left hand. His left leg was useful only for balance, being rigid and not completely flaccid. He had probably willed himself to walk again, yet this condition did not deter him from making a living for his family.

Nonno Stegel managed a drayage business in Fiume. At that time, the early 1900s, that meant using draft horses and wagons. I heard many times the story of how he was able to manage these big horses with only one hand. Usually four horses to a wagon were a handful for a healthy man. My father always described his father with amazement and respect; and this extraordinary man was my grandfather. Even though I was very young, I remember thinking about him a lot. He must have had a strong will and enough resourcefulness to want to continue to work at a job that required special skills and strength. These attributes were also instilled in my father.

As the oldest, my father assisted and then took over the business when he was very young. He was only sixteen or seventeen when his father suffered his first stroke. My grandfather's second stroke and sudden death left my father in charge of running the family business for a few years.

Just before World War I, a fire broke out in the barn, and all the horses perished. The family income was wiped out. By that time, however, most

Papa's family: Nonna and Nonno Stegel (seated); Guiseppi (Pepi), Zinka, Papa (Philip/Lippi), and Milka (standing, left to right).

of the children were able to work outside the home, and my father was required to enlist in the Austro-Hungarian army.

Papa was very close to his mother. The visits she often made to our home showed how much my father loved his mother. They acted as if they were old friends, not just mother and son. They would talk at length in their native language, Slovenian, which sounded very sweet to me. Although I did not understand the language, I could see the respect and affection my father had for my wonderful, white-haired grandma, Nonna Stegel. After Grandfather Stegel's death, she lived in Split, Croatia, with her two daughters, Zinka and Milka.

Milka, the youngest, never married. Zinka had two children and became a widow when her children were very young. Philip, my father, and Pepi, my uncle, both married and lived in Fiume.

My grandmother was always laughing and joking with us, playing simple games that only children and grandmothers enjoy. She wore large gathered skirts and always fixed her white hair in a bun. Her blues eyes sparkled with joy and some mischief, too. I would sit in her lap and she would hold my hands. Then she would chant to me in Slovenian words I could not understand and point her head to the ceiling. As I also looked up, she would open her legs, and I would fall almost to the floor in her skirts.

Her hair was silky, completely white, and her sweet face was beautiful to me. She was so fun and so loving. She could communicate well with us in Italian, but all her games were in Slovenian, and that was all we needed for our play.

My father must have had a very happy childhood, even with the difficulties, because his mother could always turn everything into fun. My father was like that in my early childhood, before the war.

They called my father Lippi and his brother Pepi, short for Giuseppe. Zia Zinka was serious and well-educated while Milka was task-oriented and quiet. All four were relatively close to the same age. The family lived in Fiume until Zinka married a banker, Zivko Rusic, who was transferred to Split.

While Zio Pepi was a colorful, lively man, Zia Milka was quiet and shy. My father told me she suffered from meningitis when she was little and had been protected during her growing years. She was content to assume the role of housekeeper for her sister's family. She did the grocery shopping every day and cooked the meals, and was comfortable with her tasks. When Zia Zinka moved to Split, Milka followed with Nonna.

Zia Zinka became a widow early on. Nonna remained in Split for a few years and lived with her two daughters, and together they raised Zinka's son, Zivko, and daughter, Nada. Both children were spoiled by the adults in their lives, I thought. Nonna, however, loved us very much and never showed any favoritism. I knew she was ours, too, but nevertheless I was a bit jealous of these cousins. Nonna Stegel passed away a few years later, not from illness but from abdominal surgery and peritonitis.

Zia Zinka had met her husband while doing secretarial work in the bank, so she resumed this work after her husband's death while Milka stayed at home. I was only able to visit them a few times while I was growing up. We children could not communicate very well because we did not speak each other's language.

Zia Zinka (standing) and Nonna Stegel (seated), with my cousins Nada (left) and Zivko.

Later in life I became very close to Zia Zinka, who could speak Italian perfectly. We sent each other many typed letters throughout the years. She was the heart of the family, keeping in touch with the family of her brother, my father. We corresponded in Italian, exchanging many thoughts.

She was the one to organize visits to Fiume, probably bringing Nonna Stegel to stay with us a for few days. It was difficult to know my cousins because they did not speak Italian and I could not understand Croatian. I could see their look of futility during our visits, but Zia Zinka was always happy and smiling.

After I came to the United States and learned English, my cousin Nada also learned English in school. She later came here as a visiting professor at the University of California, Los Angeles. We were able to get together while she was here, and when she returned to Croatia we continued to correspond.

Languages were sometimes a problem in our family. My father's mother could speak Italian and Slovenian; my mother was comfortable only in Hungarian; and in Fiume the official language was Italian when I was born. Fortunately, my father was fluent in many languages, except Hungarian. He could not speak to his own mother-in-law, who knew only Hungarian. In his later years he had a fairly good mastery of English. Both my parents could speak German and Slovenian, and managed some of the other Slavic languages pretty well; but my father could never learn Hungarian, and my mother was not fluent in Croatian. Italian was the language spoken in our family.

Later in life, when I visited Split, I observed a different lifestyle in Zia Zinka's home. The two aunts had everyone sitting at the table while they served us an entire meal. Their custom was to feed the children and guests and they themselves would eat later. In my home in Fiume, we all sat together at meals, while my mother would get up only if needed and to see that everyone was taken care of.

My cousins Zivko and Nada were very well-educated and studied until they were well into their thirties. They both played the piano and, of course, the accordion. Nada became a professor of chemistry at the University of Zagreb. She never married but later had a career in government, becoming vice consul for Croatia in Trieste (1999). Zivko studied law and eventually became a judge. He married Dessa, an orthopedic doctor, and they had two girls, Zlatka and Zinka. Their last name (Rusic) was not

Cousins Nada and Zivko, Aunts Zinka and Milka, 1955.

passed on, nor our father's name (Stegel). Brother and sister, the strongest family members, in the end had this shared coincidence.

Zia Zinka passed away while her daughter Nada was here in the United States on a professorship. Her son Zivko, very close to her, tried to call her at home during his working day. That evening they discovered that she had died quietly, alone in her home.

17 UNCLE PEPI

THE ITALIAN WORD for uncle is *zio*. To a five-year old, Zio Pepi was a wonderful, fascinating man, even if I didn't get to see him very often. When, years later, I saw the movie star Robert Mitchum, I always thought of Zio Pepi. They shared a certain similarity in manner and looks—the relaxed, sometimes distant posture and the slow smile with twinkling eyes. My uncle was very handsome and also very loving.

My father's younger brother Pepi was a truck driver and a very good mechanic. A few years earlier there had been only draft horses for transport. The fact that he could drive a big truck made him very interesting to me. No one else among our family and friends could even drive a car. There weren't any cars to drive anyway. However, even with his debonair demeanor, there was something a little sad about this uncle. It became more pronounced in later years. He loved us, the four children of his brother. I could see it in his expression of joy and fun when he was with us, but we could only see him for short moments now and then. My mother once said, "Emma won't let him come here."

Pepi's wife, Emma, was possessive of her husband. She was not very attractive, with her protruding teeth, but she knew how to dress. She could not have children so she did not want her husband to be exposed to the happiness of a family. That was what I thought then and what I still think. Zio Pepi would sometimes come by at the end of his work day and bring a load of leftover fruit, oranges and apples that were on the verge of spoiling. They were still good for us, and they were free.

He was always in a hurry, and my mother said, "He doesn't want his wife to know he is visiting us." In fact, we rarely saw them together on a visit. In their life as a couple they doted on each other and never knew the joy and sacrifice of having children of their own. They had a small white Hungarian dog with very long hair that one or the other always carried in their arms.

Emma always wore a beautiful fur coat and lots of jewelry. She was very glamorous. Zio Pepi wore a dashing leather jacket and an expensive-looking gold wristwatch, and he drove a motorcycle. I always thought people might be jealous of them, including my mother. My parents never had any type of jewelry, not even a wedding ring, but I believe they did not think the same way or believe in that style of living. My uncle's life was not involved with families, school, or activities with children. So as to not displease his wife, he visited us only on short occasions.

Zio Pepi could not permit himself to spend time with our family. A child often sees truth without outside interference. I could see that he loved us, and he loved his wife, too. He was torn between the two, and he chose his childless wife. The message I perceived, reinforced by my mother, was that he was not a man to stand on his own. He needed Emma and was easily swayed by her and circumstances.

As I recall, my mother had issues with this too, from her father's experience. He had been easily swayed by the officers of the Austro-Hungarian army to gamble away his tailor's earnings. He made their uniforms, but he was easily talked into gambling away what they paid him.

My mother seemed to see her brother-in-law and her own father in the same light. It was hard for her to understand how one person could influence another in this way. My father always responded to comments about his brother with silence. He wished it could be different, I am sure.

Life for Zio Pepi was not happy after the war. He and his wife emigrated to New Zealand, where there were no relatives nearby. He wrote to my father that he felt isolated with no family except his wife. Later he wrote to express a wish to join us in the United States. I could see that my father was very sad for his brother. He said, "Zio Pepi is very lonely, and he would like to come here to be with us."

One year Pepi and Emma planned a vacation to Italy and were going to visit us on their way from New Zealand. She really did isolate him from his family. My father became very sad and depressed after this unfulfilled promise.

Years went by, and my uncle became ill with throat cancer. His closest friends wrote to us that Zio Pepi spent a lot of time with them in the years he lived there. He talked often about his life in Italy and about his family. They wrote that he was very lonely. Zio Pepi passed on and Emma remained alone; she never made friends. My uncle's friends wrote that she would be well taken care of as the couple had been well off, with properties and other financial savings.

Sometimes in one's old age children can be disappointing, but not having children at all is very sad. Families are so important.

18 NEW HOME

AFTER THE BOMBING of our house, we were without a home, and I don't remember where we stayed immediately after that. There were several other families also affected. What I understood from the talk I heard was that there were two or three bombs that missed the target and hit the populated area. The port below was the real target.

The town authorities immediately relocated us to another part of the city where public housing had just been completed. The street name was Via Andrea Doria. Later in life I was unable to locate this street as all the names were changed and the buildings were different. We were lucky to get a first-floor apartment on the corner of the big concrete building. The apartment complex consisted of a row of multistory structures. There were two apartments on each floor.

The Dinellis lived in the first-floor apartment adjacent to ours, moved from another bombed-out area. The family consisted of a mother and her son and daughter, both in their teens. Our families became fast friends and good neighbors. On one side, the building had no windows; at the bottom, a concrete wall enclosed a piece of ground in the shape of a triangle. In this small piece of unwanted ground, filled with bits of concrete, rocks, and other construction debris, my parents envisioned another garden—a potential place for a few vegetables and even some chickens for eggs.

They quietly started to clear the ground and make space for planting. They piled all the rocks and debris near the walls that enclosed that area, making another small wall inside the eight-foot-high concrete wall. The poor soil was turned and enriched with manure and compost they collected from around the neighborhood. There were still some wagons and horses in use in the city. My mother would really feel good when she could collect a bucket of horse manure. From her youth spent in Hungary, she remembered with fondness the horses and the compost-enriched farms.

My father again built sheds for rabbits and chickens, and after a while we had reestablished a little bit of paradise in the midst of concrete. All the work had been therapeutic for them, as was the change of house. The old house had sad memories of Sergio, and this was a new project.

People in the housing development started to discover and were envious of this little place of vegetation and life. But we knew they would never have done all the work to create the garden. Instead, the area would have accumulated more and more debris and refuse. Their talk was not important because at this point there appeared more serious trouble.

One day I heard heavy steps coming up the stairs to our apartment. I saw two big German soldiers with the swastika on their sleeves. Their knee-high boots were very shiny. They had come with an open car and two more were waiting outside. They talked in high-pitched shouts to my mother, as if she were deaf. I was behind her, watching. She was speaking to them in German, but they did not give her much of chance; their voices were much louder and meaner.

I was trembling behind my mother like a little invisible mouse. They did not even see me; I did not make a sound. Mother appeared so short, standing in the doorway, dressed in black as usual, and the Germans seemed like giants to me.

The German SS (Schutzstaffel) had arrived, and they wanted my brother Ireneo. He was now eighteen, and they wanted to know his whereabouts. Their voices indicated questions, but I did not understand anything, and my mother was answering in their language. I finally saw them leave with loud, noisy steps down to the street. Four of them came back later, marching up the few steps from the street.

19 GYPSY ORACLE

MY MOTHER WAS a very extraordinary person to me. I used to look deep into her brown eyes and listen to the stories she sometimes told me during the happier times of our life. Many of the stories were of her life as a young girl in Hungary around 1900. She told me of the sounds of Czardas (a traditional Hungarian folk dance with a slow introduction and a fast, wild finish) that drew her into a gypsy camp on the outskirts of Budapest. Her family lived in the city close by. The gypsies knew her, and she visited them at times during the day when they were cooking, washing, and working around their camp. She looked like a gypsy herself with her dark skin, mahogany eyes, and long dark brown hair tied with a red and yellow scarf. Her father's family was unknown; could he have been a child of gypsies?

My mother said that gypsies were a common sight around big cities of the Balkan Peninsula. Their wagons and horses pasturing in the countryside were part of the scenery in Hungary. The Puszta, a large prairie region, was their adopted home for long periods of time.

Yolanda, my mother, loved the music of her country, typified by the Czardas that gypsies played so skillfully on their violins. But this talent was a source of superstition and fear for her friends: how could simple people without education play the complicated melodies of the Czardas? One girl said, "Maybe a devil guides their hands!"

Sometimes Yolanda was able to sway a friend to accompany her to the gypsy camp. Her friends were fearful and wary of these strange people. They had heard the old wives' tales of their psychic powers. Yolanda was fearless; she loved these people because they were different. She did not believe in superstitions, and their music was her soul's expression.

Margit Soltesz.

Her sister Margit finally agreed to accompany her one time. From a short distance they could see the campfires surrounded by colorfully dressed gypsies with their violins. On seeing the girls, they invited them into their circle to sing with them. Their songs were sometimes bursting with life and at other times so sad they could bring tears to your eyes. The evening became a crescendo of choruses and captivating music. Margit did not sing. She just listened while studying these expressive people. Yolanda was caught up in the singing, the gypsies enticing her melodious voice into one song after another.

Seeing Margit so uneasy and reserved, an old woman came up to her and asked, "Do you want me to read your fortune?" Relieved to move away from the noisy campfire, Margit followed the gypsy behind one of the wagons. With an impenetrable expression on her face, the woman looked for a long time at Margit's right palm and then her left. Then she started speaking in a low, clear, whisper:

"You are in love with a man who will betray you, and you will have a child. This man will leave you and you will suffer. There may be a tragic end that is beyond your control. Take care of your health."

Margit shivered. The gypsy went into so many small details about her life that were uncannily true. "Is Andreas going to leave me now that I will have a baby?" she thought. The gypsy watched Margit darkly, then disappeared into the shadow of the campsite. Margit returned to stand near her sister.

At evening's end, the tribe accompanied the girls to the edge of the camp and played one last, passionate melody of goodbye. The sisters chatted on the way home. Margit was uneasy but more secure with her older sister at her side. "The gypsy read my fortune and told me some things that are true. I am afraid now."

Yolanda replied, "You are just like the rest of them; you believe in nonsense. Our destiny is already planned and life goes on, as it should. You have to live the best way you can." Yolanda tried to quiet her own thoughts as well.

"The gypsy was right in so many things. I now feel a little sick." Margit started coughing and spitting up pink mucous. Yolanda looked closer at her, thinking that Margit was very pale, except for her rosy cheeks. She had recently gained unhealthy weight. Disturbed now herself, Yolanda vowed to keep a watchful eye on Margit. She put her arm around her, and they reached home safely.

Not many months later Margit had a baby girl. Andreas disappeared three months before the baby was born. It was discovered too late that Margit suffered from advanced tuberculosis. She cared for her little daughter as much as her strength allowed, but before the baby was a year old, Margit died of consumption. The child was adopted into a farm family.

20 THE STORIES OF THE OPERAS

THE OPERA ARIAS that my mother sang so often had great meaning for her. I am sure she could associate all the tragedies of the operas with people in her life. I often would hear my father talking about the irony of one opera or the satire of another. My mother seemed to focus on the tragedies. She had experienced some in her own life.

One she often sang was *Madama Butterfly*. This is the story of poor Cio-Cio-San (Butterfly), a geisha who waits faithfully for her captain, Pinkerton. Her blond, blue-eyed son is her whole world in a sad life of waiting. When the father of the boy, an American seaman, comes back to Japan with his American wife in tow, Butterfly agrees to give up her child to the couple if Pinkerton himself comes for the boy. Left alone, her last words are, "*Tu piccolo addio, tutto e finito* (Goodbye, little one, all is finished.)"

Butterfly takes up a dagger and reads the inscription, "Die with honor when it is impossible to live with honor." She gives the boy the American flag, sends him off to play, then kills herself behind a screen.

Tosca is a story of political intrigue. Floria Tosca is a celebrated singer. The man she loves, Mario Cavaradossi, is a painter and an idealist. His rival, Scarpia, is the dreaded chief of the Roman police. Cavaradossi is accused of being an accomplice to his friend, Angelotti, who is a political prisoner of the state, escaped from Castel Sant'Angelo.

Cavaradossi, whose political and religious opinions are suspect, accidentally becomes involved with the escaped prisoner, Angelotti, who hides in the church where Cavaradossi is painting. The artist is taken prisoner, accused of political treason. Scarpia, who has his eyes on Tosca, proposes to her a simulated execution for Cavaradossi, in exchange for

Tosca herself. She agrees, and Scarpia signs a "safe conduct" for Cavaradossi to get out of the country.

Tosca, after her final agreement with Scarpia, takes a dagger from
the desk as he approaches her and kills him. She then goes to get Cavaradossi, but finds he has been killed outright, as planned by Scarpia.
Tosca discovers the treachery and leaps to her death from the tower of
Sant'Angelo.

Faust is another sad story. Dr. Faust wants to be young again so he
can win the lovely and pure Marguerite. He bargains with the demon
Mephistopheles for youth. Marguerite falls in love with Faust and has his
child. Valentine, Marguerite's brother, wants to avenge the wrong done
to his sister. Swords are drawn, and Faust, aided by Mephistopheles,
deals Valentine a mortal wound. Marguerite, who becomes mad with
her misfortunes, kills her child and herself. At the end, her prayer saves
her soul, but Faust is taken by Mephistopheles to his kingdom of hell.

Il Trovatore (*The Troubadour*) is about Azucena, a gypsy who, to
avenge her mother who was burned at the stake, steals the local count's
infant son and raises him as her own. One day the count's other son and
the gypsy's son are in a battle, brother against brother. The gypsy's son is
killed and the tragedy of her initial actions is uncovered. The son did not
belong to her anyway. Retribution can have unforeseen consequences.

In *Rigoletto*, the court jester who ridicules all the nobility with
his satire and clever jokes has a daughter, Gilda, who is his whole life.
When one of the counts takes his daughter, he becomes the avenger. He
arranges for Sparafucile to deliver the count to him, dead and in a sack.
The count is a regular visitor of Sparafucile's sister. The sister, hearing
that her brother has the job of killing her count, convinces her brother to
save the count (because "he brings in money") and instead just take any
man who comes in his path.

Rigoletto's daughter comes to their door disguised as a man. Sparafucile probably never even realizes who it really is. Since she is the first
"man" to come his way, he kills her as his sister told him to. He places

Gilda's body in a sack and delivers it to Rigoletto. Rigoletto laughs—he is now avenged—until he opens the sack.

In *Turandot*, the beautiful Princess Turandot is called the princess of ice. She does not want to be possessed by any man. She has three riddles, well disguised in mysterious words, and three words that one must guess to win her: hope, blood, and Turandot (*speranza, sangue, Turandot*). Many men have tried to solve the riddles and lost their lives by guessing wrong.

Il principe ignoto (an unknown prince) finally wins her. He solves the riddles and this way she becomes his slave. He gives her one chance to be free: she has to guess his name. In the end she falls in love with his courage and his generous heart. She does not know his name, but he whispers it to her: Calef. It does not matter now, because she has decided to love him. The message here is: we cannot direct our heart—it will direct us.

All the operas have stories that could apply to today, and the music tells those stories beautifully. Like the crescendo of the music in *La Forza del Destino* (*The Power of Fate*), life is rushing river and cannot be stopped. It takes along with it all the sad and sometimes happy or funny stories.

All the stories are allegories or satires that one cannot take literally, but the hidden meaning is there for understanding human nature. My mother saw this, and the viewpoint of the operas became hers.

21 MY MOTHER

Mama in 1923, twenty-seven years old.

MY MOTHER OFTEN wanted to talk about her youth. Was it because she wanted to remember that she was once young? She had an interesting life, with times of joy but also of sorrow. One time she told me about visiting La Città d'Oro (Prague). I envisioned a golden city that someday I would visit myself. I asked her why it is called "the city of gold." She said, "Because in the evening at sunset the city transforms into gold all over." At times I could see the sadness in her face as she thought back to other times. I envisioned a city that was all gold—roofs, even streets—and I wondered how my mother walked around this city with friends. Were they happy times?

I remember her talking about it when she was in her fifties and I was just twelve or thirteen. I didn't give much importance to it at the time. I was not much inclined to listen; it seemed so far away in history and time that I could not relate to what she was saying. Later, when I could no longer hear her voice, I had the sorrow that comes from longing to hear my mother talking again and not being able to. Then, in the recess of my mind, her words filtered back, and now I can write them down.

My mother's early years were spent in Budapest, Hungary, where she was born. She remained a true Hungarian, always singing the songs of her country. She taught me to sing the Hungarian national anthem. It sounded sad, and I have forgotten the words.

She always thought and wished I would inherit her voice, which could have been very similar. Because her singing was so special and sacred to me, I did the opposite. I kept it in my memory and never sang like she did, maybe because it made me sad.

My mother told me of the great Hungarian Puszta, a wild and open land—similar to America's Wild West—where cattle herds grazed and outlaws roamed. Here the *csikos*, or cowboys, drove their great herds down from the high steppes before the harsh winter settled in. She mentioned at times one of the operas she liked: *La Fanciulla del West* (*The Girl of the Golden West*).

Gypsies, too, roamed these vast grasslands with their haunting music. They cooked goulash over open fires, roasted ox meat or mutton, and whatever they could find or even steal. Today's Puszta is protected by national parks and nature reserves.

My mother told me stories of a certain relative who was a very skilled horseman and a *huszár* (Austro-Hungarian cavalryman). She had great regard for this man and talked about how well he could handle horses. I didn't realize until years later that this mysterious and exciting man was her Uncle Andreas. His son, Albert Balogh, later confirmed for me that his father was a hussar in Hungary before he came to the United States.

My mother also told me about her mother's sister Sarah. I remember well her name but not the details of her life. Apparently she died young in the United States, and her widower, a man named Nicholas Kovach, had wanted my mother to emigrate to the United States to raise his motherless children. This was when she was young, before she was married. My mother also noted that, of all her siblings, she was the one who most resembled Sarah. Nicholas Kovach was much older than my mother. No doubt Maria's brother Andreas was involved in trying to bring someone from his family to America by arranging a marriage.

My mother always talked with longing and a sigh about this period of her life, when it was probably at a crossroads, and events were happening without her being able to control her destiny. She must have felt as if something had fallen through and she missed out on a new life adventure. For whatever reason, she moved on with her life, married, and in 1926 gave birth to my oldest brother.

She had a few years of happiness with four children, but later she shed so many tears for them. I always remember the picture she had at the head of her bed when I was small; it is almost imprinted in my mind. Now I see it again, and when I observe it, I see why she had this picture over her bed.

It is a picture is a Madonna and child. The mother is holding the hand of the cherub asleep among the bedcovers, and tears are falling on her cheeks. Did she know then how life would turn out for her and her child? The mother's face is apprehensive; it is clear that she fears what life has in store for her sleeping child. It was a dear picture then; later it became very sad. Then again, it is symbolic of my mother.

The Madonna and child image that hung at the head of Leda's parents' bed during her childhood.

22 THE HUNGARIANS

THE FOUR BALOGH siblings—Maria, Andreas, Karoly, and Sarah—
were from Budapest, Hungary. They traveled to Fiume in 1902, at a
time when the city was part of the Austro-Hungarian Empire and
Fiume was the third most important port on the Adriatic Sea. From
there Andreas, Karoly, and Sarah emigrated to the United States the
same year.

Maria had married Paolo Soltesz in Hungary. When they arrived in
Fiume they had three children: Margit, Yolanda (my mother) and Paolo
Jr. The family was to follow Maria's brothers and sister to the United
States. They later sent the necessary funds for the voyage.

The amount they sent was $500, a considerable sum in those days.
However, the quota for the Hungarians was filled when the money
arrived, so the family was obliged to wait in Fiume until the next quota
opened. Paolo found a good job in his trade as a tailor, working for the
military. Meanwhile, the money sent by Maria's brothers dwindled away
as more children were born, and then World War I began. The dream of
emigration faded away.

All the Baloghs had been born near Budapest and the Carpathian
Mountains in Hungary (before Soviet rule). Maria, the oldest, was born
in 1870. The American descendants of Maria's brother Andreas visited
the area and were unable to contact any other family descendants of the
Baloghs.

Maria's husband, Paolo, also born in 1870, grew up in an orphanage
in Kassa (also called Kossice), which later became part of Czechoslova-
kia. Information on his origins is unknown. There are no known relatives
of Paolo Soltesz.

Family legend has it that the Baloghs—Andreas, Karoly, Sarah and Maria—were children of a Hungarian baron and an unnamed courtesan. Their mother was very young, and she died after the birth of the last child. According to information from Andreas's son Albert, the baron was an irresponsible alcoholic who was prone to abusive behavior. At a very young age, Maria, the oldest of the four siblings, assumed the role the mother and raised the small family.

Andreas, in his youth, became a hussar in the elite cavalry of the Austro-Hungarian army. After moving to the United States, he married Rosa, who was also a Hungarian émigré. Rosa came to America alone, with no family of her own, at the age of seventeen. The couple had nine children, including Albert Balogh, who lived in Los Altos, California, with his wife Ruth in 1999.

Sarah married Nicholas Kovach. Their descendants live in Florida. Sarah died at a young age, leaving her husband with several young children to raise. Nicholas later remarried. Sarah's brother Karoly never married. He returned to Hungary after a few years and lost contact with the family. The Soltesz/Balogh family is descended from the Magyar (Hungarian) race and belongs to the Reformed Waldensian religion.

This Hungarian branch of the family has maintained a close community. In older times they married within their nationality. Today they own and operate an extended care facility in Palm Bay, Florida. I visited there one year with my Aunt Irene and was amazed to find that it was a little Hungarian city. The language and food were totally ethnic Hungarian. It brought back memories of my mother's cooking.

While there I met one of Sarah's children, Margaret, who has since passed away. She was then in her eighties and could not recollect much about her mother because she was so young when Sarah died.

23 THE SOLTESZ FAMILY

A PICTURE I will always remember is of a group of World War I soldiers posed together in an atmosphere of camaraderie. One of the tallest is a young blond man, my father. Close by him is another tall man with dark hair, Paolo Soltesz, my mother's oldest brother.

Zio Paolo,
c. 1917.

I later heard my father say that he would often visit this big Hungarian family, so different from his own. The Soltesz family had nine children: my mother, Yolanda (1896–1957); Margit (1897–1921); Paolo (1899–1981); Manzi, (1903–1917); Elena (1907–1973); Alika (1906–1991); Emilia (1911–1965?); Irene (1913–1994); and Arpad (1915–1918).

Margit, whom I mentioned earlier, died of tuberculosis as a young woman, and Arpad died when he was a small child. One story was that he fell on something hard and died soon after of inflammation of the brain (meningitis). No one was ever sure what caused the inflammation or whether that was the cause of his death. A fall was mentioned. My dear Aunt Irene once said, "I remember holding a little child in my lap and then he slipped off my lap." I wondered what was in her heart for years when thinking of this incident.

There was another name in the family genealogy, Manzi (1903–1917), but I am completely in the dark about her. She died as a young girl. I heard my mother talking about Manzi one time, and she was very sad and distressed. She had tears in her eyes when she said, "What a waste and tragedy." I could feel her heart aching with deep grief.

My mother's mother, Maria, could not speak Italian. To me, she seemed inscrutable. She was very imposing and good-looking, with salt and pepper hair worn in a large bun on top of her head. I wanted to touch her hair sometimes—it seemed silky—but I did not dare. I don't remember ever seeing her smile. She never warmed to us, even after all our attempts to attract her attention. She would shoo us away, then talk at length to my mother in Hungarian. She almost appeared angry; we must have irritated her. My mother did not comment on this to us, but my impression was that she tried to soothe and pacify her mother, perhaps saying something like, "They are just little girls."

This grandmother lived with her favorite daughter, Elena, of whom she was very protective, and Elena's husband and son. She only had eyes and arms for this grandson, Franco. He was about my age. I understand now that Grandmother Maria was too old and worn out to deal with any children other than the one with whom she lived.

Fate had given her many sad events in life. Her husband went missing in World War I, and she was left alone with the many children she had borne in the course of 20 years. She lived in a country—Italy—where she felt like a stranger and did not speak or understand the language. I had the impression she did not like Italy or anything about it. Three of her children died in very sad circumstances. And in her own youth she had to shoulder the responsibility of three younger siblings and a father whose own children never wanted to talk about.

After they emigrated to America in 1902, Maria's sister and two brothers lived in Chicago. They attempted to have her and her family join them. When this became impossible, the brothers planned to have Maria's oldest son, Paolo, emigrate to the United States, but then Maria's husband went missing during World War I and young Paolo had to earn a living for the family.

The next one of Maria's children chosen to emigrate was my mother. Her uncles even had a potential husband for her—the widower of Maria's sister Sarah, Nicholas Kovach, also Hungarian. He was much older than my mother, and she talked about him with sadness. The name remained in my memory, but I was too young to understand what I'm sure was a complicated story.

Because of the unavailability of telephone, all of these plans were weeks and months in formulating by mail and by steamship. The years passed and nothing was accomplished. My mother said once, "It was not my destiny to go to America. It was not meant to be." In the end, Mother married my father, Philip Stegel, whom she met through her brother Paolo.

My mother's brothers and sisters were all settled in Fiume, assimilated into Italian life. Paolo was a *vetraio* (glazier); Alika, a barber. Emilia and Elena were sent to school for a few years, which was basically an orphanage where they learned trades such as embroidery. My mother and her siblings would speak among themselves in Hungarian, but their children only spoke Italian, and none of us learned Hungarian. The only Hungarian words I remember are terms of endearment that my mother would speak to us.

Before World War II, we often visited these aunts and uncles, but as happens today, everyone was very involved with their own family life. And then, after the war, we were all displaced.

Aunt Emilia had one son, Nini (Giovanni), who was much older than my sister and me. Nini emigrated to Argentina after World War II. He became a civil engineer, and I understood he had a very good job there. Later I found out that Nini died of a sudden heart attack when he was in his forties. My Aunt Emilia (whose married name was Lucchesi) was waiting in Genoa to be reunited with him at the time of his death. No one in the family was ever able to get in touch with her afterward. I often thought that she must have died of heartache, as her only son was everything to her and she had lost contact with her husband.

Uncle Paolo and his wife, Sophia, had one son, also named Paolo, born in 1924. I never really knew this cousin as he was much older. Sophia died young, and Zio Paolo remarried in 1940, but there were no children from that second marriage. Uncle Alika had two sons, Ezio and Claudio, close to our age and with whom we still correspond. They live in Bolzano, in Northern Italy.

Franco Bogataj was the only son of Aunt Elena. Franco, Ezio, Claudio, and the children in my family grew up together and were pretty close. Franco now lives in Venice with his family, and we also correspond with him regularly.

Aunt Irene, the youngest of my mother's siblings and our favorite aunt, never married. She was seventeen years younger than my mother, who basically raised her. When she visited us, I used to hear my mother and her talk together late into the night; they would laugh and cry when they talked about their past. My mother knew a lot about the family, but I believe she shared mostly the fun times with Aunt Irene. Later in life I would ask Aunt Irene about the lost children in her family, but she did not seem to know details. Perhaps she was just too young when all the tragedies happened.

Front: Grandmother Maria Soltesz; back, left to right: Irene, Alfredo (called Alika or Ali), and Emilia Soltesz.

Aunt Irene emigrated to Canada after World War II, about the same time that my sister and I emigrated to the United States. She finished high school in Canada (Toronto) with a high school equivalency diploma (GED) and went on to become a nurse. She worked for many years in a Toronto hospital and later at Virginia Mason Hospital in Seattle. We were together until her death from heart disease in 1994. She was in her later seventies, but still so very young. I could never think of her as old. She gave her heart and life to us and was our second mother. She gave us everything and then was gone.

We have relatives in Florida and California, descendants of my mother's maternal uncle, Andreas Balogh, and maternal aunt, Sarah Kovach. It was Aunt Irene who searched them out. They are her second cousins. No doubt she fulfilled my mother's dream for her to find their uncle and aunt if possible.

24 PAOLO SOLTESZ, MY GRANDFATHER

PAOLO, MY MOTHER'S father, was long gone when I was born. "Don't mind what anyone felt about your grandfather. Let all that go, and I will tell you the real story," my mother said. An illegitimate child, he was brought up in an orphanage where he learned the trade of tailoring. Maybe because of his temperament and inclination, there was a hushed story told by my mother's brothers and sisters that he was really the son of a gypsy woman and one of the local landowners.

Since Paolo had been placed in a private orphanage that taught children a trade, it followed that he must have been subsidized by some unknown family member. Children who were sent to poor county orphanages were warehoused at minimum standards and most certainly were not trained or educated. In any case, when Paolo became an adult, he had a decent trade which became very valuable.

He moved to Fiume from Budapest with his growing family, where he became well-known to the officers of the army who were quartered there. Fiume was a bustling port city at that time, of strategic value to the Austro-Hungarian Empire. With war on the horizon, there were many officers' uniforms to be made.

Paolo had one serious character flaw: he was a gambler. He gambled away the money he earned on the very day he was paid. After delivering the uniforms he had made, he was easily tempted into any of the local taverns where he would lose his wages. One of the stories I had heard was that all the money the Balogh brothers sent for the family to emigrate to the United States he eventually lost in gambling.

Fortunately for his family, Paolo had compensations other than his regular wages. He had sewn for himself a long overcoat with many special pockets inside. These pockets were designed so that objects could be concealed in different locations. Heavy items, such as sausages, could easily be stored in the upper lining of this coat, and the pockets at the bottom of the coat held such things as bread and candies.

Paolo was a master at sneaking a few items whenever the opportunity arrived. He would come home to the family and, with a gleam in his eyes, throw his coat open to reveal a wealth of surprises. Gypsies in those days were known for stealing, but Paolo was not considered a gypsy and therefore was not watched very closely. In my home, we all laughed about and loved this story, but it was a family secret.

When World War I began, Paolo was drafted into the army. By early 1918, he had disappeared and was never heard from again. His name turned up on the long list of those "missing in action." His wife, my grandmother Maria, was left stranded. She was a Hungarian living in Italy with no extended family, no income, and nine children to raise. Her two youngest girls, Emilia and Irene, were placed in an orphanage where they grew up speaking Italian. Emilia, the older of the two, kept her Hungarian language, but Irene forgot it and could not converse with her mother.

Maria's older children struggled to make money at various jobs. Paolo, the oldest, apprenticed in a glass factory. Alika worked in a barber shop, and Elena, more frail than the rest, was talented at embroidery. She could make very precious and beautiful lace work—tablecloths and many other items—that were highly prized. Yolanda, my mother, worked in a bakery and candy shop. There were three more children—Margit, Manzi, and Arpad—who died during those difficult years.

Maria's marriage to Paolo and the birth of their many children had dashed her hope of emigration to America. Then her husband's disappearance robbed her of the chance to have a happy life.

Grandmother Maria lived an isolated life with one of her daughters. She could not speak Italian, and she did not seek contact with anyone other than her family. I was never able to be close to her and she never talked to me. But I had another grandmother who made up for it.

25 A Portrait

THE BEAUTIFUL OVAL face, the penetrating, lively dark eyes in this portrait show an animated personality. The date of the photo may have been the early 1900s, considering the style of hair, a type of page-boy cut. Her figure was beautifully formed; she could have been an actress.

It was my Aunt Emilia, who was a fascinating person. She had big brown eyes and dimples, and a smile that was full of life. She had so much energy, and it seemed like she could do almost anything. She had only one child, a boy named Nini, who was much older than my sister and me; he was in college when we were both under four. Emilia was very close to him, and they would go hiking in the mountains and take many excursions on his motorcycle. I often looked at the picture with Nini driving the bike and my aunt sitting sideways behind him, the Alps in the background. No doubt she had bought the bike for him. Even with her job and her son, she still had time to sew many dresses for us.

Carnevale in Italy is a little like Halloween in the United States, but it is celebrated in February—for most of the month. In the streets of Venice especially, it is normal to see people in costume, going to their jobs and other activities. The Carnevale of Venice is famous for the elaborate costumes—people trying to outdo one another. The atmosphere is happy at this time. Carnevale is celebrated all over Italy. Similar to Halloween, children like to wear all kinds of costumes, but they do not go collecting candy.

My mother was not one to participate in fun things with us. Her life had already known considerable tragedy, so my Aunt Emilia tried to compensate for her. I remember that she came to our house like a whirlwind one day, with crepe paper, ribbons, and thread. She cut out petals and leaves from rough crepe paper to make a flower. She used my mother's sewing machine to stitch a beautiful skirt of round red petals, layered to form a poppy, and a black top with puffy short sleeves. I actually did look like a poppy, with a green hat cupped over my head.

She had another plan for my sister Wilma, who was blond with blue eyes. Wilma was going to be a bachelor button. Aunt Emilia cut bright blue crepe paper in long, thin petals that formed a skirt with green leaves as a background. The top was white and simple. This skirt was even more spectacular than mine, and there was an elaborate blue, layered hat. My sister became a beautiful flower. I remember that even our faces were painted in a colorful way. Zia Emilia sewed on Mother's Singer machine with a continuous droning that would stop only briefly now and then. She would take a quick measurement of the waist, then go back to the machine, with her hands flying over all the several layers of strong crepe paper. This was accomplished in a short time, and we were ready for Carnevale.

Later in life, Zia Emilia did not match what this portrait represented to me then. She raised her son, Nini, to be everything for her, maybe because something was lacking in her marriage. My cousin was a handsome young man, very dashing on his motorcycle, and the pictures of the two stopped at a scenic spot on the road to the mountains, appeared so happy and so perfect. They were happy, and it was the best time of their lives.

With the help of Zia Emilia, who always worked at a good job, Nini was able to graduate as an engineer from the university. I know that at one time in her life, when Nini was grown, Emilia and her husband separated, and she remained alone. After the war, Nini emigrated to Argentina where, still young, he died suddenly. He was trying to bring his mother to Argentina. At the time, Zia Emilia was in Genoa, waiting to be reunited with him. After Nini's death, she became completely detached from the family and was not heard from again.

26 PAOLO SOLTESZ, MY UNCLE

MY MOTHER'S ELDEST brother was Paolo Jr. When their father disappeared during World War I, he had to take over the support of the family. Paolo was a good-looking young man, tall with black hair, dark skin, and regular features. In another picture I saw him in the military uniform of World War I.

What I remember is much later than that. Zio Paolo worked in a glass factory. It was fascinating to see him cut glass for a window with his magical tool. Paolo had one son with his first wife, Sofia, whose name was Paolo, but they called him Puccio. Sofia died when very young, and then Zio Paolo married Tina, a much older woman (or so it appeared to me). They never had any children. I was so much younger than Puccio that I can barely remember him as a quiet young man. First the illness and then the loss of his mother when he was just a child must have made a sad imprint.

I was very fond of all my mother's brothers and sisters, and I remember well all their different personalities. Their spouses were not as close to us, and I remember Tina especially because I felt she did not like us. She was not able to talk to her young nieces and nephews and seemed to regard us as strangers.

As often happens with some men and women, Zio Paolo went along with his wife and did not try to maintain relationships with the rest of the family. After he remarried, Zio Paolo did not keep in close touch with us, and we only saw him occasionally. When we did see him, he always had his wife at his side. He appeared to be holding back his emotions with us, unlike most people who hug and talk to children. His wife was the main person in his life, and even his son was not close to him.

Even today I wonder why we restrict ourselves to just one or a few relationships rather than love everyone who comes into our life, because love is generous and knows no bounds. To remember this is happiness. "Happiness is like being at home," and home is our heart.

I visited Zio Paolo later in life. After World War II he lived in Rome with Tina. In the confusion of the war, we lost touch for a long time. Then one year, with my sons Corey and Chaney, I went to Italy and met Zio Paolo again. He was happy to see us. He and Tina lived in an apartment in the center of Italy. Puccio lived in Milan with his wife and son. Zio Paolo could tell me very little about my much older cousin, never having been close to him, and seemed to have little contact with him.

Paolo and Tina had only each other and together spent most of the time in their apartment, drinking wine and smoking. Paolo worked in a bookstore, but Tina just sat at home and corresponded with some of her relatives in Yugoslavia. After Paolo died, she went to live there.

27 MY BROTHER IRENEO

MY BROTHER IRENEO (1926–1945) was a quiet type, very thoughtful and unassuming. From the age of sixteen he had been working as a *modellista* (modeler) in the same shipyard as my father. His name

Ireneo, c. 1942.

was based on the name of my mother's youngest sister, Irene. It was an unusual name that was only used in official papers. The everyday name we used was Pippi. I never knew the origin of this nickname, but it was very dear to me. Years later, when I saw a movie with Tom Hanks, I saw Pippi, with his blond hair and blue eyes, and his silent gaze that knew so much.

I was ten years younger than Pippi. When I was only about four or five years old, he seemed very tall, at least six feet. His expression, when he looked at me, was extremely soft and tender. I would often sit in his lap and just look at him and feel very secure. I don't remember talking very much. My mother was worried about my late start talking. I heard later that she took me to the doctor about this, and he laughed, saying, "Signora, you just wait, and she will talk too much!"

When Pippi came home, he would often sit in the kitchen, where my mother was fixing dinner. While they talked, I would just look from one to the other while I nestled in his lap. Ireneo had nearly perfect features—his nose and eyes were perfectly symmetrical. Most of all I loved his warm, direct gaze. He could look at me for a long time without blinking. Was he thinking he had to keep me well in his memory for the future?

His voice was not loud, but that of a young man, soft and clear. He had a very special relationship with our mother. I observed the way they talked, Mother busy with dinner, Pippi talking quietly about his day. I think he was also trying to be of comfort to her after the recent loss of our brother Sergio.

My sister Wilma, two years younger than I, was busy with small toys on the floor, so Pippi did talk to me a little more. Many times he came home with special gifts in his pockets: little doll furniture, such as a table with chairs, a cupboard (China cabinet), and a sofa with fabric already glued to the seat. "Look what I brought you. Do you like it?" he asked with joy and sparkling eyes.

Being a model maker in the shipyard, he was able to build small furniture on his lunch hour at work using little pieces of wood. He could design and build anything, because that was his special talent and training.

Mama and Ireneo.

Schools are different in Italy. There are five years of elementary school, then three years equivalent to high school here. After elementary, one could choose to go the route of higher education, which would involve three years of high school, *scuole medie*, plus five more years of college. Or a vocational student could choose the trade route with three years of high school, *scuole commerciali*. After that, additional training would be needed as an apprentice in a definite trade. My brother was thus a qualified *modellista* at age sixteen, working for a small wage.

After World War II began, I saw a change in Ireneo. He was restless and anxious. After a while, his peaceful and patient presence was gone. He was not around us much as usual. I thought for a while that he was working late and leaving early in the morning.

One day I was sure he did not come home, and I never saw him again. I missed him and longed for his warm hugs, the toys, and the secure and peaceful feeling in the kitchen. Now I sensed why he always looked so deeply into my face. Did he have a premonition about his life with us?

I finally accepted and understood that he was where he felt he should be. In fact, he had chosen to join the resistance movement rather than be recruited at age eighteen into Mussolini's Fascist army.

The war years were uncertain. We had been bombed out of our home. In our new home, I remember, my mother received a letter from Pippi, not in regular mail but hand-carried. The orders from Pippi were "to read and destroy the letter" so as not to incriminate the family.

I heard my mother talking to my father. The letter was sad. Up in the mountains life was hard, cold, and fatiguing. I saw my mother's tears. She said, "I don't need the letter anymore. The words are sculpted in my heart. They will always be there."

28 SILENT MOVIE

THE WAR WAS in full force, and now the Germans and Fascists were united. All men age eighteen and over had to join the Camicie Nere (Blackshirts, members of armed squads under Mussolini). Pippi had to choose between the Fascists and the guerrilla bands in the mountains of the Venezia Giulia, Italy's northeasternmost region, which juts out into the Adriatic near Fiume.

My brother was just eighteen. His heart had been in turmoil, as I had sensed. It was a hard decision: enlisting in the Fascist army or going into the mountains and leaving his beloved family. My parents knew he had gone to join the resistance movement. But the secret that he was gone could only be kept a short time.

The Germans were at our door now. I heard the clicking of their boots coming up the few steps to our apartment in the big housing development in Via Andrea Doria. My mother and I were alone in the house. My sister was next door visiting Signora Dinelli, our good neighbor who was always taking Wilma in, giving her cookies and spoiling her. My sister would spend entire days there with the Dinellis.

The two Germans who came to our door seemed huge to me, their heavy steps echoing in the stairwell. Their knock on the door was frightening. They had metal helmets and the swastika on their sleeves. They had a pushy presence and were talking very loudly, almost shouting. My mother was answering their questions and talking to them in German. As I hid behind her, I heard the soldiers' rough voices becoming louder and more intimidating. My father was at work and could not protect us.

I was watching this frightening scene like a silent movie; I could not understand anything. They were not going away, and then my mother, without explaining, sent me over to the Dinellis. She said, "I have to go with them, and you stay here with your sister until I come back." She did not explain any further, and I could see she was very fearful and anxious.

Mother was taken between the two soldiers to the headquarters, where she was actually arrested. Nobody was notified. When my father came home from work, he learned from the neighbors what had happened. He went immediately to the station where my mother was being held and negotiated an exchange.

Now I knew that my brother was a partisan and this was the reason the Germans had come to our house. Pippi had not enlisted in the Fascist army, and the Germans were unforgiving. However much they despised Jews, they hated "traitors" or rebels even more.

My mother came home the next day, but not my father. I am sure they had to go through a thorough investigation. They finally agreed to let Mother go home in exchange for my father, who was held hostage for my brother. Mother and I went to the prison many times for visits, but we accomplished nothing. The process of interrogation was a military routine that took a few weeks.

The Germans must have had some intelligence that my brother was a partisan. I know of one instance where a mother hid her son underground out in the country and he was saved, as was his family. My parents' statements that they did not know where their son was did not help. The Nazis grilled them and shouted at them.

Without notification or warning to our family, my father was sent to Germany. He spent the rest of the war at hard labor in a political concentration camp. This was not a death camp—there were no gas chambers or ovens—but the prisoners lived in unheated barracks surrounded by barbed wire and received very little food.

There were many concentration camps in Germany—all of them dehumanizing. I don't remember the name of the camp where my father was sent, though I would recognize it if I heard it mentioned.

In one final attempt, Mother demanded to know what had happened to him. The German officers were scornful and even amused by my mother. Their policy was to withhold any information about prisoners. One of the officers was a tall blond man with handsome features but a cruel smile. He told her, "We don't know where you husband is!" He spoke in Italian with a thick accent, even though he knew my mother could speak German.

We left there with my mother leaning on me, tears running down her face.

29 Borsa Nera (Black Market)

MY MOTHER WAS very sad; now there were only three left of our family of six. The fate of my father was uncertain, as was that of my brother. Did she foresee a future of more losses? She was mostly silent. I was also very quiet, talking minimally, unlike most little girls. She may have had too much grief to share with and burden her child. At this time, near the end of the war, I was eight.

Our neighbor Signora Dinelli finally came to our rescue. She gave my mother a good talking to about her duty to care for her two daughters. Talks were never shared with us children, but sometimes I was able to sneak around and hear. I kept everything to myself and never asked questions, maybe because I felt helpless and was not encouraged to talk.

After a while, Mother gathered some courage and her spirit seemed to lift a little, especially since Signora Dinelli gave her a job. The job was to take tobacco and other goods to exchange with farmers for potatoes and other vegetables. She had to find out what was needed and what could be exchanged. This involved a lot of bartering. Signora Dinelli had a little store in her house.

During this time, Mother risked her life. She had to go to the farms in outlying villages, and the only transportation was the train and walking. A lot of trains were being blown up.

When she would leave, my sister and I were the charges of Signora Dinelli. But eventually I realized what my mother was doing and I insisted on going with her. Nothing would stop me, not even repeated spankings. I would not physically let her go without me. Even Signora Dinelli could not tear me away, and I would cry very loud and run after my mother as soon as I could wriggle free from our neighbor's grip. A few times I just went like that, tagging along; then I was outfitted with a smaller backpack, which was heavy, full of goods.

We would leave early in the morning together. We would come back late at night, alone in the dark streets, loaded with packs of food. Signora Dinelli was always ready to take everything that same night, and Mother would bring home food to feed us. We had no income at all. The apartment was public housing, probably with very low rent. There was no such thing as public assistance, as there is today, for a family without a wage earner.

That is how we survived during the war. Like my dear Slovenian grandmother said, "*Manje ali slast*" (less but sweeter), and we felt lucky.

30   LIFE OF PERIL

MY MOTHER BECAME close friends with Signora Dinelli. This interesting woman was a wheeler-dealer in many ways. She had a tiny store in her apartment where she would buy, sell, or trade anything of value. She made enough money to take care of her family, a son and daughter both in their late teens.

The son, Renato, was unable to work because of a debilitating bone disease, so he was studying for a college degree in design or architecture. He had to walk mostly with crutches, sometimes with a cane when he was feeling better. He was also a dedicated sculptor, and we still have some of his marble art.

Lea, the daughter, had an office. The three were very close, and in this instance I could really see that "blood is thicker than water." Lea had a fiancé, but I heard that after many struggles between them they separated because Lea would not leave her mother and brother.

Sometimes I watched with fascination as Signora Dinelli weighed sugar, flour, or potatoes on her big steel scale. She measured with great precision but then would throw in an extra potato or add a little more sugar.

My mother was one of the people who brought goods to sell. I knew my mother risked a great deal in this venture, but this was all she could do when my father was gone and she had to provide for her two remaining children. The *borsa nera* (black market) was a way of life and a means of survival for many others besides ourselves.

In the struggle between the occupying German army and the Italian guerrilla bands, there were many trains blown up, especially at night. These were the little local trains that my mother had to take to get to the countryside where she bartered with farmers. In her backpack she would carry clothes, blankets, cigarettes, and other things the farmers needed. She would come back with much heavier loads, her backpack filled with potatoes, corn flour, turnips, and many other goods. She was a very good trader.

Now and then I heard people say, "Another train blew up last night!" My mother was aware of the danger, but she had no other choice. She had faith that we would be lucky. We had to survive, and there was no other income. Sometimes the two of us had real fights, but I would not let her go alone. She tried to sneak off sometimes, but I would wake up, grab my bag, and run after her. Our trains never blew up during the day, although those same trains were sometimes derailed during the night.

31 THE PSYCHIC

WHEN WE MOVED to our new apartment, my sister was five or six and I was two years older. Signora Dinelli lived across the hall in our apartment building where our two units faced each other. She became very close to my mother right away, as if they had been old friends. I never knew her first name, and as children we never called any older person by their first name. It would always be *signor* or *signora*, *signorina* if not married.

Signora Dinelli was a widow who brought up her children Lea and Renato all alone, which was rare. Most families in Italy have many relatives around them, but the Dinellis had only themselves. There was an older son, but he was living in New Zealand. Lea, very athletic and a good-looking blonde, was engaged a long time, but it did not work out, and her fiancé left her. Renato, also a striking young man, never planned to be married with his condition, which they called tuberculosis of the bones. He was always very busy with studying, drawing, or sculptures. Later he became an engineer and worked for a big company near Turin.

Besides trading goods, Signora Dinelli also read tarot cards, but only on special occasions and only for certain people. She was a true psychic. She could anticipate my thoughts without me saying anything. Everything in her house was so interesting and busy.

People were coming and going, bartering and selling goods they could not find or afford at the regular store. Signora Dinelli was able to sell things like cigarettes for less, and some things were just not available outside her store. This was all due to the black market, or *contrabando* (smuggling). It was somewhat secretive, but maybe only secret from the government.

Tarot card reading was also a good source of income for Signora Dinelli, but she would only *butta carte* (throw cards) when she felt so inclined. During these times we were not allowed in her house. It was one of her rules that children were not to be present during her card reading.

Signora Dinelli even looked like a witch—a good witch—as she often took care of us. She limped as one leg was much shorter than the other. She had gray-green eyes, penetrating but benevolent. Her blondish white fine hair was in a bun, but flew all over anyway. Her nose was short and turned up, with wide nostrils from frequent use of snuff. She blew her nose often after the snuff, and followed that with much sneezing. She always had her big white hankie in her pocket. It seemed to me that she snuffed every time I looked at her. She was meticulous in her habits, and her dresses were always very clean. She wore an apron that covered most of the dress and would brush off any snuff that got on her clothes.

Once she read the tarot cards for my mother, probably at my mother's insistence. Later I heard my mother talking to a friend about it. Signora Dinelli was reluctant to read cards, especially with my mother, who may have had some unhappy omens; but she tried always to tell only the good things.

"She told me she saw me up on a hillside walking slowly; the hill was a grape orchard," I heard her say to another housewife. "She said I was picking the white grapes, but these represented tears."

Mother talked about other details of the reading, and I know it disturbed her; but she had insisted on it herself. I knew Signora Dinelli was remarkably good with those cards, as I had heard other people talking about it with amazement. She was also very careful about not saying bad things, but people always read more into it.

Signora Dinelli often took care of us after my mother started bartering and traveling to the farms. She was probably the main person who pulled my mother out of her severely distressed mental state. During this time there were no aunts and uncles visiting. We were all alone in a new apartment at a time when the families of our aunts and uncles were also struggling.

Anyone who associated openly with partisans' families openly risked being killed by the Germans. My Uncle Ali also was sent to a concentration camp, I later found out.

32 THE JEWS

THERE WERE MANY Jews in Fiume being rounded up by the Germans and held prisoner in buildings in an area between Fiume and Sušak. Fiume was not a huge city. My mother knew some of the Jewish people there. She was also known for being kind and fearless, and so took on another job. Some who had relatives in the camps asked her to take items—mainly food and clothing—to their relatives being held there. Unfortunately, these were only halfway destinations: from here people were sent by train to concentration camps.

I remember going on these trips with my mother, taking baskets of food—sandwiches and cookies lovingly made by relatives. We both would carefully carry a basket so as not to disturb anything it contained. Mother almost acted as if we were carrying gold.

Walking side by side, Mother and I presented ourselves to the guards of the building. She spoke in German, asking them to deliver the baskets to those whose names were on the bundles. The baskets were taken and, we hoped, delivered, but we never saw the inside of the prison. The huge gate was closed and the guards were posted outside.

Once or twice, the guards turned us away, baskets and all. I sensed that the people they were intended for were no longer there, having already departed for Germany. I could not understand anything that was said in German and my mother seemed unable to explain to me. She must have been too upset to articulate the fact that these prisoners had been sent on to the death camps in Germany or Poland. After a lot of talking, my mother would turn back silently and my chin would drop on my chest as we slowly walked away.

However, my immediate thought was that now we had to walk back to Fiume with baskets full of food, and I was usually very hungry. After a little while I asked Mother if we could look in the basket and see if there was something to eat. She would finally open one of the bundles and give me part of a cheese and salami sandwich. I can still taste it—it was so good. Mother would not eat anything; she just walked silently and looked very sad. She would not have the heart to tell those who sent us that the baskets had not been delivered because their family members were already gone.

This is how Mother was able to decide to give me food from the basket. She usually would take me home and I never saw her meeting the families on our return. Walking beside her, I could feel what was going through her mind, and I understood when I saw her tears. The relatives of the Jewish prisoners had entrusted their precious food from home for her to take to the prisons, because they could not take it. They would be arrested themselves if they took it to their brother, father, or son with goods from home. They trusted my mother with this task.

She was not afraid to risk her life for these poor people, suffering in the camps. The Germans were systematically arresting all Jewish people. They also brought death on people aiding either the Jews or the partisans. These people were regularly executed. Farmers in the outlying villages were also executed for hiding or aiding the partisans, even if they were only suspected.

My mother was a friend of the Jews and must have been pretty good at talking to the guards in German, as they did not treat her badly. I remember they were just young, grown kids who may have seen her as a mother. She was happy when they would take the bundles and promise to deliver them.

The Jewish people were grateful to her and slipped some money in her pockets, though she did not ask for anything. She told me they all would cry together and console each other, sharing as they did the cruelty of an insane war led by insane people.

33 SILENCE ON THE BRIDGE

EXCITEMENT WAS IN the air. I could hear voices all around me, in one side or the other of the big apartment complex and in the street. Everywhere echoed an excited tone of voice. As I went outside the house, I could hear distant cries. Children were running excitedly toward downtown, crying out, "*La guerra e finita, la guerra e finite!* (The war is over, the war is over!)" I stood still, just listening, as the voices faded in the distance.

Downtown was not very far from our apartment, just a few blocks, and I also ran there after I understood the festive atmosphere. I wanted to see the excitement, but Mother was quiet in the kitchen and not moving. My sister was with the Dinellis and not moving either.

The Allies were driving up the main street of Fiume in their jeeps, tossing candy and gum and wrapped chocolates. All the children scrambled while the adults crowded close to the jeeps and trucks, trying to hug the soldiers as they were going by. It was so exciting, and I was full of joy. I came back home to tell what was happening in the streets. My mother remained quiet.

The excitement lasted for a few days as people were mingling with the GIs in the town, watching them as if they were from another planet, and pouring love on them. We loved the "debonair" look, their smiles, their energy, their easygoing way. As a child of nine, I watched them with awe.

My mother was not involved in the celebrations. Even when she went downtown with me to see the Allies, she only watched silently, far from the crowd. She was apprehensive. My father was still in some unknown place in Germany, and my brother was in the mountains with the partisans.

My sister was usually in the care of Signora Dinelli, so Mother and I one morning started to walk in the streets that led to Sušak Bridge, the border between Italy and Yugoslavia. I remember our arrival at the square in front of the bridge and the details of the scene there. The typical "piazza," where several streets entered from the city, was full of people. On each side of the bridge there was a cyclone fence, but the gates of the bridge were wide open. The river separated the two towns, Fiume and Sušak.

The Sušak Bridge, looking toward Sušak, c. 1938. Photographer unknown.

Over this bridge, groups of partisans were passing, ragged and dirty, either in groups, in twos or threes, or alone. They were members of the Stella Rossa, a brigade of partisans from that region. As they crossed the bridge and came into the piazza they would increase their pace, then run to some waiting relative. The piazza was filled with small crowds, and everyone was looking anxiously at the bridge. The fortunate, reunited, would walk away happily.

Mother and I were standing a little way from the bridge under the shadow of a huge tree. It seemed to me as if we were almost hiding and didn't belong to that crowd. Mother was quiet, her hand on my right shoulder. I was just nine and many times she had told me how I was just the right height for her to lean on. I was her faithful cane. Mother had been injured as a little girl and almost lost her leg. She had been caught under the wheel of a wagon after a team of horses spooked while she was walking to school. She limped all the rest of her life because her knee had been fused in place after the accident.

Because of her limp, she always leaned on my shoulder when we walked. This time she was leaning especially hard on me, as if to get comfort as well as support. I was only as tall as her waist and couldn't see her face while we were walking, but I looked up once and saw tears streaming down her face.

At this point it was not just her physical handicap that made her lean on my shoulder so heavily—it was the premonition that her son was not going to be there. She needed the warmth of my shoulder, the assurance that she still had a child with her.

Signora Dinelli had interpreted a dream for my mother a short time earlier. In my mother's dream, she was on a hillside picking white grapes and looking at them but not eating. Signora Dinelli interpreted the dream this way: "You will be shedding bitter tears for a sad incident that happened in the mountains." This is what I heard, and it remains in my memory. In my heart I also knew that this trip to the bridge was futile; seeing my mother quietly crying told me she knew it too.

In the corner of the piazza, the two of us were waiting. I had a strange feeling of isolation and sadness, but I said nothing. Separated from the rest of the people there, Mother was only watching the bridge. We stayed there most of the day. There had been some rumors for some time that my brother had been involved in a confrontation with the Germans—nothing official—and it was not discussed with family or friends.

The number of partisans coming home was dwindling, and finally at evening time only a very few were coming through. They all looked very tired. They had walked a long way from the mountains. They all had suffered cold and hunger while on continuous alert. Finally, Mother had the courage to go to one of them and ask, "Did you see my son. A tall blond boy (*Un giovane biondo*)? His name is Ireneo."

"*No, Signora, mi dispiace* (I'm sorry)." He shook his head, as did the others that followed. Most of the partisans knew each other, but they acted as if they didn't know. Maybe they did not have the heart to tell my mother the fate of my brother.

I felt an emptiness inside me and an indescribable ache all through my body. I looked up at my mother's face and saw her tears. She quickly wiped them off with the back of her hand. I said, "Mama," and put my arms around her. I couldn't help but cry. She didn't say anything; her throat was choked up, but her eyes told me not to say anything now. We hugged together. I cried so much. We were alone, had nobody but each other, and there was nothing I could do because my pain for her was even greater than my own.

It was getting dark, the piazza was empty, and everybody had gone home. Mother and I, all by ourselves, finally turned to go home. We walked slowly, looking back a few times, but the bridge was empty. I kept my eyes on the pavement, while Mother leaned on my shoulder more firmly, more for comfort than support, and I tried very hard to hold back my tears. I was her only comfort now. I had to be strong. The premonition that her son was not coming home made me more aware that she needed my shoulder for warmth and assurance; that was the reason she had me with her. I was glad now that I did not let her come here without me.

Signora Dinelli, the psychic, had tried to gently interpret Mother's earlier dream. The white grapes in the mountain. . . . She was known for her accurate foretelling of future events with the tarot cards. Now it came back to me.

The war was over. But it didn't matter now; that was unimportant.

34 PARTISANS

THE GERMAN ARMY was relentless in attacking small towns and the countryside where they suspected partisan activities. The partisans shifted their locations in the mountain areas all over Italy. They were always moving from one area to another, and the people of each area were always helping them.

The Germans regularly made raids on these villages. Sometimes they would line up a group of people against a wall and just execute them, only because they were suspected of harboring a partisan. It was true that the people were allies of the partisans. Some were neutral, but sooner or later they would assist in one way or another.

There were very few men in these villages, and most of them were old. All their young men had already gone to the army, either Italian army or with the partisans. I know of one instance, however, where a mother managed to hide her son underground all during the war, thus escaping either side of the fighting. Her son escaped the danger of war, but many more did not.

Jack Olsen, a Pacific Northwest writer who was in the U.S. Special Forces, documented the war in his book Silence on Monte Sole. This book relates what happened in the area near Bologna, which was attacked by the Germans. Other areas in the mountains were also attacked continuously in an attempt to wipe out the partisans.

As mentioned earlier, in Istria and Venezia Giulia, where my brother was fighting, there were large groups of partisans under the name of Stella Rossa. These brave groups were hiding in the mountains and caves of this area and had a hospital set up in the woods. They used a river to evade the Germans and their dogs. Partisans would carry their wounded a long way on their shoulders across the river and into the mountain hospital. The dogs could not follow the scent, and the Germans would have to turn around and retreat. There were also many partisan women; one became well known because she was also a doctor who came to help the wounded.

Today there are landmarks and memorials in these areas—I believe the forest hospital is also preserved—to help people remember how much hardship these guerrilla bands endured. They had little ammunition while the Germans had many types of weapons and equipment, including trucks carrying loads of soldiers armed with grenades, machine pistols, and machine guns.

I remember seeing soldiers around town with grenades in their belts and machine pistols, which they used to execute people. I can still remember the sound of those rapid-fire guns. The casualties among the partisans were great, but they had the villagers' support in the same manner that the concentration camps prisoners had the sympathy of the farmers around the camps. There are memorials of this war everywhere.

35 IRENEO

EVENTUALLY, AFTER THE war, my mother learned how my brother had been killed in the hills of Istria. After placing my sister and me in secure lodging (orphanages) arranged by our clergyman, Pastor Guy, she went on her quest to find out what had happened to my brother. She did this before she knew whether my father was dead or alive.

She went to the farmers of the area around Buie, and they were able to report all the details of what they had seen as they watched from their bolted homes. They had word that the Germans were about to make a *rastrellamento* (roundup), and they locked themselves in their homes. From the windows they saw the Germans advancing with *carri armati* (tanks), working their way up through the mountain village. The partisans were all over the area. The Germans were numerous and aggressive.

My brother and another boy were assigned to the promontory to defend the retreat of the partisan group. They were to keep the advancing Germans at bay while the larger group of partisans were escaping. The plan was that before the Germans were upon them, they also would escape.

The Germans advanced quickly with heavy gunfire, killing one of the retreating partisans. My brother and his comrade remained on the hill with two machine guns and limited ammunition. Suddenly, when their last cartridge was used, the Germans were upon them. From below the little hill, the Germans held them down with their guns, which were big enough to blow up the whole hiding place.

The two boys held their arms up to surrender. The Germans discussed the situation for a few minutes among themselves, then the leader give the final order: "Shoot. These are the real traitors."

The farmers who witnessed the event did not spare any details: the two boys were machine-gunned down across the chest. Two brave members of the Stella Rossa were dead. The priest of that village, along with the villagers, buried the two youths in their cemetery.

My mother's grief was inconsolable. She went back to Fiume and obtained a truck. Returning to Buie, she had the two bodies disinterred, then carried the remains to Fiume in the back of the truck, sitting between the two coffins during the two-hour drive back. There she arranged a funeral, which was reported in the papers. Now the two are buried in Fiume in the cemetery reserved for the partisans and members of the resistance movement. Others in Ireneo's group are buried together in the same area, among the vast number of partisans' graves.

36 THE FUNERAL

A PROPER FUNERAL was arranged with our pastor for both of the young men who died together. My mother was not going to let them be laid to rest without proper recognition of their bravery and sacrifice. All the relatives and friends of the two boys were walking behind the two caskets, and many more people created a procession of sorrowful people. They walked with heavy pace along the dark avenue of the cemetery, immersed in their thoughts in a quiet procession under the weeping willows, pines, and boxwoods that lined the avenues.

Subdued whispers of prayers could be heard, and the air was impregnated with the perfume of thousands of chrysanthemums and other flowers. In the cemetery, among the marble stones, the people shared memories in honor of those who had passed on.

In Italian cemeteries, all graves have a fixed time period with an expiration date, after which the remains are removed to a mausoleum or communal grave. The grave space is then used for another departed for a period of years. However, the graves of the partisans will be left untouched and preserved for generations. Their marble stones with the red star stand among hundreds of those who fell for their ideals of a better society.

The funeral of my brother and two other youths, Germano Zorzenon and Poscagni, was covered in the local newspaper. Below are translations of these newspaper articles.

Last Salute to the Comrades
Zorzenon, Poscagni, and Stegel

In an atmosphere of an emotional gathering yesterday in our cemetery, the funeral of comrades Stegel, Zorzenon, and

Poscagni unfolded in a solemn ceremony. Besides the civil and military representatives present, there were hundreds of citizens who wanted to convey a last goodbye to three young victims of the barbaric enemy.

The shipyard workers who had been employed with the fallen Zorzenon and Stegel were among the throng of people at the memorial funeral. A group of these shipyard workers, directed by Engineer Venucci, sang with inspired sentiment La Preghiera Dei Trapassati *(The Prayer of the Dead). This song aroused strong emotions in the people present. Particularly significant was the fact that this shipyard choir sang yesterday for the first time after twenty years of forced inactivity.*

Engineer DeLuca and shipyard worker D'Aziglio gave two brief speeches memorializing the sacrifice of the fallen and renewing on their graves the promise to continue the course of the ideal of a new social pattern in the name of these who have given their young blood generously.

Poscagni, Zorzenon, and Stegel, comrades in faith and combat, will remain in the memory and gratitude of our people.

Heroes of the People

In the heat of the struggle for liberation, the young, incapable of saying no to servitude, left to become partisans, defying the power of the oppressor. Among them was Ireneo Stegel ("Pippi") and Germano Zorzenon. The first, seventeen, was inexperienced in the military; the second, twenty-six, a veteran of six years in the navy. Both were animated by enthusiasm for true freedom and social justice. They were faithful to the ideal and the cause until the very last.

The day of 7 August 44 signaled the end of their battle. There, on the pleasant hill of Istria, with fifteen comrades, long before dawn, they posted themselves to wait for the enemy. They waited in a pine forest over the main road. The Germans and Fascists came, well-armed in several trucks and tanks on their way to a roundup.

The attack was immediate and effective, but in light of the large number of enemy troops, the partisans had to retreat. Ireneo and Germano were entrusted in the rearguard to protect the retreat of their comrades with their machine guns. And here they fell, accomplishing the duty of soldiers of the people until their last cartridge.

Today, two years since this event, their comrades remember them and their parents weep in sorrow, who loved them so much and lived long months in prison and concentration camps, uncertain of their fate; and all their friends bring to their graves the flower of their gratitude.

We remember, comrades Stegel and Zorzenon, your serene and sweet expression, the faith always in your heart, your generous soul ready for sacrifice. Faithful and humble heroes, you admonish us with your example that human life acquires the real meaning and real strength only in following to the end the way and ideals that our conscience imposes on us and our heart ardently desires.

To the Fallen

Following the sacred tradition of all the people, Fiume commemorates its fallen today. Our country enjoys the first warmth of the sun and of freedom. But for the warmth of this sun, they, our heroes, have consecrated their existence.

We have not abandoned their remembrance, not even for an instant. They have accompanied us in the cold winter nights when the desire to rest would give shivers to the weakened body from hunger and exhaustion. In the summer afternoons, with great tension, they waited for sinister steps. In the mingle of gunfire and blood, in the painful tortures in the police rooms, they came without waiting for our tired voice. With their lips they kissed our wounds, as angels.

They have touched our shoulders, with their soft hands, to let us know we do not think of them as empty shadows. Their eyes, bright with light, have encouraged us when strained from grief; with teeth clenched from the pain, we wanted to stop the fight for our goals. They encouraged us to continue to our end, on their very own path, the white course of sacrifice and victory.

Our fallen comrades did not die but are more than ever alive: they are in front of us, and they guide us. We did not cry for their death because they live in us, in our hearts, in the joy of the children, in the serenity of the old, in all that is valued in our life.

Chrysanthemums on the Stones—
Day of the Dead (Memorial Day)

The saddest memories today are forming deepest wounds of sorrow in our hearts. A faraway mourning in the past comes to the surface again and surrounds us with sadness and heavy meditation of the fragility of humankind. A recent mourning exacerbates this desperation and brings more tears.

A noble tradition requires that this day is consecrated to our departed, and to all the dead. On the hills that lead to the cemetery of the people, hundreds, even thousands of people are bringing to their departed ones the greeting of a prayer and the gentle homage of symbolic flowers.

Flowers, on that barren ground, on the wooden crosses, on the headstones, and the marble, stand out in multiple colors with their warm beauty in contrast to the cold rigidity of the tombs.

All the dead! So many, after this inhumane war, are still mourning, and not all are resting here, under the cypress of Cosala [the Fiume cemetery], in the heart of the very earth that had given life to them. Mothers, wives, and children were deprived by the horrible ferocity of the apocalyptic conflict of the comfort to weep on the grave, ever so humble, of their fallen. Their grief is today bigger than ever, as a flooding river.

All the dead! The hate that has caused so much grief in the body and spirit—joins on this sacred day in the conscience of the universal grief that is equal to the suffering of a terrible plague, and torments the whole world. And we place also on the cold grave of an unknown enemy lacking affection, a generous flower as a thought of mercy and forgiveness.

Slowly they walk, a procession of women, men with grave, slow steps, the children timid and silent, in the dark aisles of the cemetery. They seem immersed in mystic thoughts. Above them the lanterns, the weeping willows, severe pines, basswoods, and the cypress, form the great corridors of the cemetery.

Slow and subdued can be heard the whispering of the prayers, and all around the air is impregnated with the acute perfume of thousands of chrysanthemums and other flowers. But it is not only among the marble of the tombs in the cemetery that the memory is touched in honor of the departed: in every home and in every family is celebrated the religious solemnity of this day.

Today, every remembrance is a prayer.

37 CAMPS

THERE WERE MANY concentration camps. The worst were the Jewish "death camps"—Auschwitz, Dachau, Treblinka, Birkenau. There were also "work camps" where political prisoners were made to do terrible jobs, such as clearing the bodies out of the gas chambers. If they refused, they were executed themselves.

My Uncle Alika was a barber by trade. His shop in Fiume had been a gathering place for men who were against the regime and wanted to talk about politics. These discussions were done in secret, but sooner or later the Germans came to know about this.

Uncle Alika became a political prisoner and was interned in a camp in Germany where his job was to shave heads. The Germans did everything in their power to separate families, so my father, my uncle, and all of their friends were systematically assigned to different camps. They didn't learn of each other's fate until after the war.

When the war was over and the camps were liberated, my father looked like a skeleton and was lucky to have escaped death from starvation or disease. There was a lot of dysentery, and many people died in the political camps.

With the war's end, all the prisoners began to walk out of the camps. My father started his walk from Germany to Italy. Often he was able to get rides from Allied soldiers passing by. When he finally reached Fiume, he was in rags and unshaven, just skin and bones. I was not home at this time, but I later saw pictures of him taken for his identity card. The man in those pictures didn't look like my father at all, but rather like a derelict.

The reason I was not at home when my father returned was that my mother, uncertain of the fate of my father and brother, had arranged for me and my sister to stay at an orphanage. She could not take care of us two girls when she was in such a desperate state of mind. In fact, the minister may have arranged for someone to be with her out of fear that she was suicidal.

After he returned, my father seldom spoke of his experience in the camp. I heard fragments of conversations later on. He talked about the farmers who raised potatoes in the fields outside the camp. These people were kind and generous to the prisoners and helped them survive. These camps were not as strictly supervised, so the prisoners could slip through the wire at night and glean potatoes from the fields. The farmers knew this and let them take anything. They would cook the potatoes on open fires, and this aided their survival. I heard him say; "German people were good. It was their government and military that were destructive."

In fact, I never heard my father show any hint of prejudice for any kind of people. All I remember is the equality he so desired for all. He often said how it was necessary that all people have equal benefits and equal rights in life.

38 REVENGE OF THE PARTISANS

ON THE EVENING of April 25, 1945, Benito Mussolini and Claretta Petacci, his lover, were fleeing from Milan, trying to escape into Switzerland. They attempted to reach "La Valtellina," a region near the borders of Piemonte and Lombardia. The partisans caught up with them on April 27 at Dongo, near Lago di Como, and placed them in a farmer's house overnight, in Bonzanigo.

Almost all the farmers were allies of the partisans, helping by hiding them, giving them food, or reporting information of the German strategy. Many villages were discovered helping the partisans, however, and many of these villagers were executed by the Germans. People helped at the risk of their own lives.

On April 28, "Colonel Valerio" arrived from Milan with Aldo Lampredi (called Guido). During the war, Valerio was a pseudonym of Walter Audisio. Both men were well-known leaders of the group of partisans called Stella Rossa. The two leaders had several partisans with them, members of the band. All the different bands were bitter adversaries of the Nazis.

Benito Mussolini and La Petacci were taken by automobile to the nearby village of Giulino di Mezzegra. Here, in front of the gate to the estate of Villa Belmonte, they were shot. Valerio, as executioner, had trouble with his machine pistol, which jammed. This was a gun manufactured by the Germans, light, small, and usually effective, which had been captured in quantity by the partisans. Another of the partisan band handed his own machine pistol to Valerio as a replacement.

According to legend and witnesses, Claretta was not in the plan for execution, but she declared she wanted to be with Il Duce. Whether it was an emotional response or fear, she went to Mussolini's side, and they fell together under the volley from the German gun.

After this double execution, the bodies were taken to Milan to be hanged upside down in the large piazza. I recall that, even as a small girl I thought what a terrible scene that must have been, but this was the payment to Mussolini for his alliance with Hitler.

In Italy, after the war, all weapons used in World War II were destroyed, part of the protocol for all war weapons recovered. A recent article in an Italian paper reported that a former partisan revealed on his death bed the location of the gun that killed Mussolini. It was recovered in a church and indeed appears to be the same gun used by the partisans. The director of the local museum begged the authorities to preserve this gun as a museum display and not destroy it.

39 ARRIVEDERCI, FIUME

AFTER THE WAR ended, our family as we had known it was gone. Everything was in confusion for me, and it seemed that nobody had any idea of what the future would bring. Pastor Guy came to our home many times to talk to my mother. I don't remember being included in these visits, and no explanation of any kind was offered. I had a feeling of great apprehension.

I only knew that some plans were being made and that events beyond my understanding and control were moving quickly. Looking back, I realize now how important it is to include children in planning that affects the entire family, regardless of how serious the situation may be. I had a feeling of great insecurity and the uncertainty that comes from being surrounded by change, with no information on which to form an idea of what was happening. I trusted my mother, and I knew that she would do what needed to be done, and I never questioned her decision; deep down I knew I had to go along with these plans.

My sister and I were suddenly on a train, leaving Fiume for Trieste, our first stop. Pastor Guy, his wife, and three children were also with us. I didn't know where we were going. Now I understand that the pastor had arranged for us to be cared for while my mother was struggled with a serious mental condition, where she could not cope with life. By this time, she knew for certain that my brother had been killed. She had no way of knowing if Father was dead or alive, or where he could be. Nobody really knew what happened in the concentration camps; people were in the dark as to what was really going on there.

The stop in Trieste was fun. The highlight was to be treated by the GIs to a pastry party for the five of us children, probably arranged by a troop chaplain. The pastor's children and my sister and I were seated around a table, and all the wonderful pastries were passed around on a platter, American style, for us to choose one. Soldiers were all around, coming and going. I am sure that, looking at us, they had quite a show.

I had never seen anything like it—pastries of different kinds I had not tasted before! We each had a little plate, and as the tray would go around we chose one to eat, and then the tray would be passed again. All the kids were just eating and ready for the next tray that came around, except for me. I was actually hoarding them all on my plate, just waiting for the next tray, so I could choose another one.

The pastries were so beautiful and so different. I have no idea now when I was going to start eating, but at some point the tray passing came to an end. Then all the other children with their empty plates started to look at my plate full of pastries. To my surprise, they all came and picked one of the pastries off my plate. They must have thought I could not eat them. I just sat quietly with a long, serious face, seeing all my pastries disappear, and I knew that it served me right. The lesson: he who waits too long, loses out.

The long train ride to Florence was memorable. All five of us children and other people were crammed together in open cars. There were no bathrooms, and we were allowed off the train only at scheduled stops. I remember we had to relieve ourselves many times on the rail bed, either when the train was moving slowly or if we had time to step down. Once when I could not hold it anymore I climbed up boxes to the edge of the train and hung out over the side.

We children were not allowed to step far from the train lest we be left behind at the station while we were the pastor's responsibility. The trip seemed interminable to me, with many stops in small towns.

We finally arrived in Florence, and I was taken to a large house where I would spend the next two years of my childhood. Wilma and I had been sent to "children's shelters" where Pastor Guy could find room for us. The one in Florence was a center sponsored by the Waldensian Church.

Wilma was taken to an orphanage near Rome. It was part of "E42," an area with large buildings that had been developed by Mussolini years earlier, then abandoned, and later converted into an orphanage.

The orphanage in Rome was much worse than mine, as I found out later. There were a lot more children there; Wilma contracted head lice, and all of her thick blond hair had to be shaved off. She was only seven years old, and the place was very hard for her at such a tender age. She had always been protected by Mother, aunts and uncles, or the Dinellis. Now she was in a very controlled situation with maybe a hundred other children and no personalized care or special attention. She was just another child there.

I was somewhat luckier.

40 LIFE IN AN INSTITUTION

IT WAS CALLED a *collegio*, but also an *orfanatrofio* (orphanage). Perhaps a luxury house at one time, the building had been donated to the church for charitable purposes. It was located in an affluent residential neighborhood not far from the center of Florence (Firenze). Across the intersection was a park with large, beautiful trees. I loved trees, as I do now, and I felt protected among them when walking to school.

The* collegio *in Florence. Francesco Bini photo

Most of the children were not orphans. Most of them seemed to have relatives or some family members who sent them packages. There were fifteen to twenty girls of all ages. The youngest were four and five and the oldest, eighteen. I was about ten. The older girl may have been the daughter of the institution's director. She had a room of her own. She played the piano skillfully, a result of many lessons, and no doubt came from a family that was "better off." I had a feeling that a better life was in store for her.

My life here seemed alien to me because I had been accustomed to the freedom of our family on the outskirts of Fiume. I had great anxiety and sadness stemming from the loss of my two brothers, the struggles of our family trying to stay together, my mother's absence, and my father presumed dead. I became unnaturally quiet and withdrawn among all these girls.

Florence was like a "foreign" country to me. I wonder if this is how many children feel when they go to a foster home—abandoned, at the mercy of strangers, like they don't belong, and as if they are in a dream that hopefully will end when they are reunited with their families.

Life here revolved around this new home and the school I attended. We walked in a little group through the park and to the street where the public school was situated. On the way back, I would see street vendors with their tables full of either food or objects to sell. My favorite table was where they cooked the *castagnata*, a pie made of chestnut flour that I found very delicious. When my Aunt Irene sent me a little money from Milan, I could buy a piece.

I don't remember any teachers in particular there; I was just a number in the large classroom. One teacher, however, did bring me out of my seat one time by inviting me to the blackboard and asking me to point to the city I came from. This was something out of the ordinary for the children who had lived in this city all their lives. My hand pointed to Fiume, and a mental picture was snapped. I was a rarity and incomprehensible to children who stayed with their parents all their life. I was a foreigner who came from a faraway place.

One time, walking back from school, I found 500 liras on the street. There was no way to find the person who had lost it, and with that money, for a few days, I was able to buy a piece of chestnut pie after school. I was always hungry; that wedge of pie hit the spot.

Occasional trips into the city with the older girls gave me the opportunity to see the cathedral and other points of interest in Florence. But on the trips to the dentist I had to walk alone. This was my first experience with a dentist.

Shortly after I arrived at the institution, the supervisor reported the sad state my teeth were in. I had a bad odor in my mouth and a lot of toothaches. My parents were not available to make decisions, so it was arranged for me to go to the dentist. I was ten years old and I didn't know anything about dentists. All I knew was that I had big holes in my teeth and they had to be pulled out.

I had to make these trips through the streets of Florence several times because I had more than one tooth to be pulled. I remember being

The Piazza Massimo D'Azeglio, through which we walked to school. Wikimedia Commons

able to put my tongue deep inside a tooth or two, and there was a bad taste in my mouth. The totally decayed teeth were pulled easily and without local anesthesia.

It was traumatic to have teeth pulled, and I became very fearful of dentists. At the time, I assumed that this was normal procedure, or maybe the teeth were so far gone that the dentist did not think anesthesia was necessary. It was still a grisly experience, but perhaps the dentist was giving free services as I had no money to pay for it. The visits and walks to the dentist office left me in state of shock all the time. I felt totally alone in the midst of people, almost like I was in a daze.

41 MY LIFE IN FLORENCE

THE ENTRANCE TO the two-story house was a large, heavy double door that opened into a marble atrium or hall. To the right were big rooms with double doors, one leading into the dining room and another to a room used for activities such as sewing and embroidery. There was a piano where we gathered around to sing—mostly church hymns.

The dining room had a long table and chairs and wooden counters with cabinets below. The activity room had only sparse furniture, mainly chairs and some tables. On a wall there were small cubicles, similar to lockers, for the children's personal things. To the left of the entrance was a hallway leading to the kitchen, where we were not allowed.

The most impressive part of the entrance was the wide marble staircase near the kitchen entrance. This led up to the second floor, where it ended on a circular landing that opened to doorways leading to the bedrooms that served as dormitories. There was one bathroom upstairs and a second, smaller bathroom on the first floor, which was a long, narrow room. Often we had to wait our turn to use one of the bathrooms, and we had only a few minutes before somebody would be knocking on the door. Perhaps that was why we all had to take *olio di merluzzo* (castor oil) on a regular basis.

The upstairs bedrooms each had a small balcony with French doors, and the iron railing had an elaborate design. Some of the bedrooms faced the street, while others overlooked a wonderful garden. Many times I would come back from school and go hide on the balcony to watch the swallows playing in the sky. I would go to dinner, then come back and watch the sunset, with the swallows going back and forth by the balcony. I would cry and cry for the freedom I had lost, for my mother, my family, my home, and my city. I thought constantly about my parents and Fiume and how it would be when I returned. I would say over and over, "I have to go back to Fiume," just like Dorothy in *The Wizard of Oz*.

But I had never heard of Dorothy, and the homecoming never happened like it did for her. I didn't see Fiume again until much later, and then I could not even find the street where I had lived.

42 VIA SILVIO PELLICO

THE *COLLEGIO* WAS on the Via Silvio Pellico. Diagonally from the big house was the Piazza D'Azeglio, a wonderful little park in the middle of the city. The *collegio* must have been a villa at one time, completely enclosed with cement walls and a large iron gate. Many girls of different backgrounds lived here under the supervision of two women. We never saw the cook or other people working in the kitchen.

The older girls would all stay together as friends. They did not include younger girls in their circle. They seemed to have a lot of things that they could only talk about to each other.

Packages from America arrived occasionally. These were big events. Large boxes of clothes were placed in the main hall, and we were all able to find some clothes and shoes that fit us.

It was so much fun, and we all needed clothes badly. I could not believe it when I found a pair of shoes that fit me perfectly. I was happy just to know that somebody else had feet like mine in another part of the world, and I felt lucky to have the shoes.

The clothes I found in these boxes from America were the best I ever had, and I wondered about the girl of about nine or ten who wore them before me. I was very thankful. The clothes were probably collected in churches and nonprofit organizations to help people affected by the war. They were a godsend. I totally wore out the clothes and shoes I had arrived with. Silently I thanked the person who donated the clothes.

I often thought about how wonderful it was to have these clothes, and I wondered what the girl who had worn them was like. I was sure the girl in America was the same size and same age as me. I was slightly taller and larger than most of the other Italian girls my age.

We sometimes had visits from GIs who brought us cookies, candies, and gum. We never would have had these treats otherwise. The soldiers seemed happy just seeing us all excited when they came to the home. We were very impressed by them, and I watched them smiling as they came in with their gifts. I just silently watched the men from America, a country I never knew anything about, except from the adventure books I read written by Emilio Salgari.

I saw something for the first time in my life that I thought was very wonderful: a viewer with slides of America. When I clicked the little viewer, another scene would appear on the screen. It was magical for me, and it would only come with the *Americani*. The magical night lights of cities, streets, and very tall buildings were astounding to me. The cities were unreal, and the scenic areas really did seem like something from another world.

Most of all I remember the GIs' energy and enthusiasm, their happiness at seeing us happy. Some of the older girls seemed to fall instantly in love with them, flirting with them. I heard them later discuss all the details of the Americans' features and manners. They acted as if they were in love, and they kept their discussion among themselves, excluding the younger kids.

I was also curious about the GIs, and one of the major things I observed was that they were always chewing gum. This seemed kind of cute and very unique because we had never heard of or seen gum before. It was so very American. The visits with the GIs were brief, which was a good thing. Otherwise, the girls would have really fallen in love, which would have been followed by disappointment. They were only about fourteen or sixteen.

My favorite person at the *collegio* was an Ethiopian girl of about fourteen named Acquadoro. She was tall and very slim, with beautiful features and African hair. She walked like a princess of the Nile, so straight and so proud. When she cut her own hair, I collected it for a doll pillow. I did a lot of hand sewing for a doll. The hair cuttings made a very fluffy pillow. Acquadoro was amused and happy to give me her hair. She didn't talk very much, and she had an accent—maybe she didn't know Italian very well.

Acquadoro was very reserved and appeared mysterious to me. She never talked about her family, but I had a feeling that she might be from the upper class, maybe a princess in Ethiopia. She looked down on us as if we were her subjects. She was taller than most of the girls.

Once, when Acquadoro's mother came for a visit from Rome, I could see that she, like her daughter, was very tall and slim, and also very silent. She wore a type of turban and a different style of dress with fine fabric draped over her shoulders. She appeared sad to me, never smiling. I wanted so much to be close and talk to her, as I would have with my own mother, but she moved away every time I tried a friendly gesture.

Many years later I learned that Acquadoro's mother suffered from tuberculosis and died a few years later. I also found out that the daughter contracted the infection and died of the same disease.

I don't remember the backgrounds of the other girls. I was the only one from faraway Fiume, while they were all from the same general area in Tuscany. Their families sent packages, and one time I was amazed when a girl said she was eating *uccellini*, which turned out to be a pastry or pasta with meat baked inside. This was a typical food of the area. All the children were not familiar with the part of Italy I came from, and it was hard for them to understand where the city was located, but they sensed that my family was too far away to send food packages. I was the hungriest girl there because I did not receive packages of food and goodies like the other girls. Their little lockers were packed with items that they could nibble between meals.

Even though we had three meals a day, I was always hungry. In between meals my stomach was growling. One Sunday after church I saw the helpers bring in the spaghetti and sauce and place it on the counter in the dining room. Dinner was not being called, and I kept peeking through the crack in the door and smelling the delicious food.

The doors were closed, the room was dark, all the shutters were closed, and everybody was in the activity room. While all the others were occupied, I sneaked out and slipped into the dining room.

The spaghetti sauce was in a separate dish in the dark dining room. I speculated how I could get a taste of it and put my fingers in the bowl. Just at that moment, the director, a tough and imposing woman, came in, turning the lights on. I hid my hands behind my back, but she was furious and ordered, "Show me your hands!" I slowly brought my hands in front of me, one covered with sauce. I received a severe scolding and punishment in the corner of the room, and part of my meal was taken away. I was ashamed and upset. It was very embarrassing for a while, but children forget easily.

The day after I had committed this crime, another incident occurred in which I behaved more favorably. The director announced that *il ricovero dei vecchi* (the old folks' home) had invited two of the girls from our home to spend Sunday and have dinner with them.

All the girls started talking at the same time. One said, "I am not going to be with those old people." Another declared, "They have big noses and no teeth." They scorned the idea, giggling and making fun of the oldsters. I felt sad for the old people who were probably looking forward to seeing children and young people. Their feelings would be hurt if nobody came to their Sunday dinner.

At the risk of ridicule, I suddenly found my voice: "I will go."

The other girls made fun of me, as I had expected they would, talking with a voices of old people and mimicking them in gestures: bent over, making terrible faces. I was the only one willing to go to the home; nobody else would venture with me, not even for moral support. This was an event they had no desire to participate in, and they weren't interested in pleasing anyone there at all.

As it turned out, when I got to the home, the old people were very happy, and they treated me like a special guest. After the wonderful dinner, which I felt fortunate to have, they had a little program, and at the end of it they nominated me *reginetta dei vecchi* (Queen of the Old People). There was a trend in those days to nominate a queen of "something," such as the "Daffodil Queen" here in the United States in Tacoma. I was indeed the little queen of the day, a ten-year-old who won a popularity contest among the sweet old people of the home.

I came back to the *collegio* with many little gifts: coloring books, pencils, and even some clothes they had bought with their limited money to present to the girls at the orphanage. I was happy; it was a fun and wonderful day. After all, while I was there I got all the attention from at least twenty people, each trying to hug me and love me. When I came back to the *collegio*, I actually acted like a queen, with all my gifts to show. I felt exuberant, in contrast to my usual serious manner. I was, after all, the *regina dei vecchi*! The only other times I felt so happy and lucky were when I received the occasional package sent by Aunt Irene from Milan and when the packages from America arrived.

Happy times such as these made life in Florence a little more bearable for the two years I was there.

43 THE VACATION

THE GIRLS AT the orphanage were allowed to leave on summer vacation if they had relatives or friends they could visit. My mother was still in Fiume, healing from a breakdown. My father was still missing in Germany, so I had no place to go.

Some families affiliated with the church volunteered to care for those of us in such circumstances. One family living on *un podere* (a farm) near Siena invited Acquadoro and me to visit. We were about the only ones who didn't have any place to go when school was out. I am sure the director herself wanted a vacation, so we were taken to the farm to spend some time with this family.

I was about ten years old by then, and my recollections of details are hazy. I knew that I had no family to support me or any other plans, and I was just being "farmed out." My Aunt Irene in Milan was the only one interested in my welfare, but she was very young and trying to support herself with very little money and no home of her own. She lived with the family she worked for.

However, I was excited and looking forward to a new adventure in the country. I was grateful that a family was willing to take us for a few weeks in the summer. I remember a farmhouse on top of a hill surrounded by barns and storage sheds. As in medieval days, most of the farmhouses were on top of a hill, and the fields below were very visible at all angles from the top. There was a vineyard on the hillside and fields of other crops and numerous fruit trees. Closer to the house there were vegetables and flower beds, and dozens of chickens were roaming free.

One afternoon after the midday meal I started to explore. I was all alone and it was very quiet and very hot. This was a time of siesta for the farmers. I entered the dark entrance to a big barn. When my eyes adjusted to the gloom, I could see a dirt floor covered with straw. In the middle were several large buckets covered with a fine white mesh. It seemed very mysterious. There was a pleasant fragrance in the barn. There were at least twelve or more of these buckets, and they were placed in an orderly manner. It made me think something very important was hiding in them.

After cautiously walking around to see what else could be happening in this dark place, I went to one of the buckets. I lifted the mesh, and there was gold! It was so yellow and smooth, it might have been gold dust. The buckets were filled with golden honey. I started eating it, dipping my finger in the gold and I ate as much as I could, then I replaced the mesh and planned to return the next day. What a windfall! I never seemed to get enough to eat, and the honey gave me a lot of energy. I thought the farmers would never miss the little that I ate.

The following afternoon was again very quiet and still hot, so I headed back to the "honey barn." I hadn't even started to eat any of the honey when I heard a voice from far away. There was a stillness in the huge windowless building. I listened carefully. The voice was faint, as if from a great distance, but I could just barely hear my name; then it came a little clearer, "Leda! Leda!" I never knew of anyone else with my name. It was a rare name in Italy, unknown except in mythology. There could only be one person calling my name.

I thought I was imagining it. Then the voice came nearer, and finally I knew—it was my mother!

She had started calling from way down at the bottom of the hillside. As she climbed the long, winding road to the farm, she kept calling my name. When I finally was certain it was my mother, I ran down the hill and around the bend of the road where I found her with tears in her eyes. My mother had finally come to bring me home!

She had gone to Florence where she was told I was at this distant farm. She had traveled two or three days from the coast of Yugoslavia to Florence, then to Siena, and then into the countryside. She had to take several trains and walk long distances between railroad stations, all the time trying to find this farm, which was not near any village. But we would have found each other no matter what. Such was our secret link: nothing could really separate us.

44 ZIA IRENE

Irene Soltesz, 1939.

WHILE I WAS in Florence, my Aunt Irene was one of my few con-
solations. By sending me a package whenever she could, she made me
feel like I was not abandoned. I used to wonder how she could guess

so exactly what I needed most; underwear and such things as colored pencils and drawing paper. I treasured the little gifts of colored pencils. It was at this time that I drew a picture of a golden retriever and sent it to her. I later found out that she kept it throughout her life.

The Italian word for aunt is *zia*. Zia Irene was our closest, most beloved aunt. She was born in Fiume on December 14, 1913. When I was born, she was in her twenties while my mother was in her forties. She was the youngest surviving child of Maria (Balogh) and Paolo Soltesz. Another child followed her, Arpad, but he died in his third year. When their father disappeared during World War I, the two youngest children, Irene and Emilia, were sent to live in an orphanage while the older children had to find work to support the family.

Zia Irene, a very sensitive child, was totally ignored by her mother, who, as I recall, was not a verbal person nor an affectionate one. Whether because of the language barrier, overwhelming difficulties, or her very nature, she was distant and disconnected, totally uncommunicative. I remember wondering as a child if she did not like us because we were girls.

After the orphanage, Zia Irene went to work for a rich family in Milan. She did their shopping, cleaning, and errands. The family treated her well, even as their own daughter, but she was at their disposal for all their needs. Even though she was not living her own life, she did not mind. Maybe it was because she had some other special people she lived for and saw once or twice a year.

She and my mother, Yolanda, were very close, so her sister's children became like her own children. As her oldest sister, seventeen years older, my mother had been everything to Irene in her childhood, giving her the love she did not receive from her own mother, including while she lived in an orphanage.

It is hard to describe this amazing person, Zia Irene. I remember her vividly, from the time I was three or four. At that time, she lived in Milan and worked for a family of Russian nobility who were fugitives from the October Revolution. She was dedicated to this family, but again, there was no opportunity for her own education or personal enrichment. The best years of her life were given to this family, who became dependent on her for all their needs.

Zia Irene never married. Later she told me there had been one opportunity but it did not work out. Her youth must have been very sad. She told me once how she would watch the city at night from her window and cry. She said she did not know why, but I know that she was crying for the life that she was missing. She never talked about her past, but this was a moment of togetherness we shared later in life.

As a little girl, I looked forward to her visits. She knew exactly what to bring us—the special clothing that could only come from Milan. She would bring dolls that we would not have had otherwise. Zia Irene was a wonderful gift to us. She loved our family so much. Her visits from Milan to Fiume were special. For days we would talk about her coming. She took all the pictures we have of our childhood; otherwise, we would not have had any. She was the only one who had a camera. With our family of four children, our parents were overtaxed and had no time or money for cameras or store-bought clothes or toys. My mother made all our clothes on her prized Singer sewing machine. Not many people owned one of those either—they sewed by hand.

Zia Irene would have made a wonderful mother, but she lived for and shared with my mother. Later, when my mother died in 1957, she became our "mother."

World War II interrupted her visits from Milan and our happy life. Even then, though there were hard times, I remember receiving some wonderful packages from Aunt Irene during the two years I spent in the orphanage. After the war, Zia Irene made it possible for my sister and me to emigrate to the United States by taking care of the paperwork my parents were unable to manage. They could not bring themselves to fill out papers to relinquish their two remaining children.

Irene knew in her heart that it was in our best interest to leave Italy. Immigration law would not allow her to come with us because she was a

Aunt Irene, 1959, Toronto.

Hungarian citizen—even though she was born in Italy—and, unlike us, was not considered a refugee. Immigration quotas allowed her to go only to Canada. She would not be able to be close to us, but at least she would be closer than my parents. While living in Toronto she worked toward receiving a GED and then trained to became a licensed practical nurse. She loved her work in the hospital in Toronto. Her adjustment to the new world was much more difficult than ours, because she was older.

Later, because of the love she had for us, she left Canada and all her friends there to take a job at Virginia Mason Hospital in Seattle, Washington, so that she could be close to where we lived in Tacoma.

As a nurse who loved her work, her world was all about people. In her private life, she cared for the ill and lonely and for all the people with whom she came in contact. She was also an artist, and her paintings were another expression of her life. She would give her paintings to people who asked for them. She encouraged other artists and influenced them in doing good work. Zia had a generous spirit and with her modest earnings, still gave to the needy.

She was a rescuer of stray cats and even birds that came to her windowsill. Most of all, she was always there for my sister and me.

45 Villa Vittoria

EVENTUALLY, MY FATHER returned from Germany. His journey from the prison camp to Fiume, most of which was on foot, took two months or more. When he finally arrived, he was a practically a skeleton, having had little food along the way. It was 1945, and I was in Florence at this time. He and Mother started to put their lives back together. They, as well as hundreds of other families, made plans to leave Fiume for political reasons.

Fiume became part of Yugoslavia under the regime of the dictator Josip Broz Tito. My father and brother had not suffered and fought for a dictator. Houses were taken over as property of the state, and people were being forced to abandon their Italian citizenship. The Italian language was no longer to be used in the schools or for official matters. Anybody who stayed in Fiume had to accept Yugoslavian citizenship and give up many freedoms they were used to. The emigration process was under way soon after the war ended, and our families became scattered.

Uncle Alika and his family went to Bolzano in northern Italy, where he was able to open his own barber shop. Aunt Emilia, with her husband and son, also went to Bolzano, where she found a job at the post office. Aunt Elena, with her husband Giovanni, son Franco, and Nonna Maria, went to Marghera near Venice, where Giovanni found work in a factory. Uncle Paolo went to Rome with his wife, where he was employed as a caretaker in the large Waldensian church there. His grown son, who had a wife and child, went to Milan with an opportunity to work there. My father and mother went to Pinerolo near Turin, where my father could use his shipyard skills in a foundry. The arrangements for our family and Uncle Paolo's family were made by Pastor Guy of our church in

Fiume—the same man who had provided care for my sister and me right after the war when my father was still missing. Aunt Irene was in Milan, where she had lived most of her adult life.

Uncle Pepi, my father's brother, moved to New Zealand with his wife Emma. My father's sisters, Aunt Milka and Aunt Zinka (widowed a few years earlier) with her two children, stayed in Split, Dalmatia, where they had lived for many years.

Shortly after his return from Germany, my father left for Pinerolo, in northeastern Italy, to find a place for us to live. He found a farmhouse where our former neighbors from Fiume, the Dinellis, were already settled. At this point my sister and I returned from the orphanages. We had been gone for two years. I had completely lost the accent of our native city and was then speaking as a Florentine. Mother could not help but laugh when she heard me talk with a "strange Italian" accent.

In times of disaster, people offered housing as well as they could. I'm sure this farmhouse was not in use at this time and was then rented to people coming into the area. It was a typical two-story house where only the upstairs was lived in and the downstairs was given over to storage and animal shelter. The upstairs farmhouse was divided into two separate apartments sharing one bathroom.

My mother was not happy with this arrangement, even though we had good neighbors. As she did with all her concerns, she went to Pastor Guy, who was also a refugee from Fiume, now assigned to the Waldensian church in Turin. Thinking back, I believe she wanted to be isolated from the togetherness of our previous life, to find peace for her soul.

The region of Piemonte has the largest population of Waldensians in Italy, and the rest of Italy may not even know this fact. In those days, Catholic Italians did not understand any other religion, except in this particular area of Italy. There had been some persecution of the Waldensians here in the past. The Waldensians had come to this refuge in the Alps to practice their religion many hundreds of years

Leda at Villa Vittoria.

before. The Waldensians, or *Valdesi* in Italian, were the first believers in freedom.

Pastor Guy was able to find us a new space in an old villa which had not been used during the war years. It was located a few miles from Pinerolo, almost in the mountains.

In normal times, Villa Vittoria most likely had been used as a summer vacation place, while at other times its owner lived in the city. In Italy, it is customary for a wealthy family to have a retreat in the mountains or on the seashore. Italians usually take all of August for vacation as well as the usual holidays.

This villa sat on a hilltop on the road to Sestriere, an alpine ski area in northeastern Italy near its mountainous border with France. Below the villa was a small village named Riaglietto. A little dirt road not far from the village led us past an old flour mill where the wheel still turned in the small river coming down from the mountains. Past the mill, the road crossed over a wooden bridge before coming to the large iron gates of the villa.

After passing through the gates between large concrete support columns, we entered the road belonging to the villa property. This road became steep shortly after the entrance, with only two concrete strips for the wheels of a car. About half a block long, this driveway led to a large four-car garage: a concrete structure with a roof serving as a terrace surrounded by railing. The view from the terrace to the valley below, with the mountains in the background, was spectacular.

Another stairway from the terrace went up to a higher level of small terraces, the largest one being on top of the garage, then gradually up the hill, with steps to much smaller areas opposite to each other, offering more views of the countryside. After this garage area and all the different levels, there was a short, steep path to concrete steps ending at a level garden in front of the house entrance.

This formal garden in front of the house had been neglected to a point where flower beds were no longer visible. The grass that had taken over was high and brown. In the middle of the garden there was a pond with scarce lily pads, a dry fountain, and a crumbling concrete statue of a woman holding a vase. There was barely any water at the bottom of the little concrete pond.

Another concrete terrace near this pond overlooked the valley, but overgrown trees obstructed most of it. There were fruit trees, but the only one producing fruit was a persimmon. In the summer it was loaded with wonderful large fruits, ripening on the branches. This must have been truly a paradise in better times.

The three-story house was designed for a single family. At ground level was a small, separate apartment where the middle-aged caretakers lived, a couple with no children. On the other side of their quarters was the kitchen for the villa's owners, with a circular stairway leading up to the dining room. I could imagine servants coming up with their dishes of food.

On the main level of the house, from the garden leading to the double-door entrance, one entered a large round hall. On the right were locked rooms where the owners had stored their possessions. On the left of the hall were our family's quarters. At the center of the hall, there was a marble staircase leading upstairs to the third level. On this floor were bedrooms, the only bathroom, and a small kitchen. This space was already occupied by another refugee family, a mother and her grown son who had been placed there by Pastor Guy before we arrived.

Our assigned area consisted of a single large room, at one time the dining room. The room had French doors opening onto a spacious sunroom, a glass-enclosed veranda that wrapped around two sides of the house in an L-shape. At the northern end of the veranda there was an ornate billiard table. This area faced the back garden, the grotto, and the forest behind the house.

The caretakers' quarters had a kitchen and bathroom. With no bathroom in our own place, my father had to improvise an outhouse—a privy in the yard. We made the best of it.

Villa Vittoria, as I understood, belonged to a well-to-do family that had not been able to use it because of war shortages. It had been empty and virtually abandoned for years. The caretakers had been left as guards but had not maintained the property. There was a vineyard below the house tended by a farmer, but during the times he worked in the vineyard he never talked to us or anybody else. The vineyard was well cared for, however, and the grapes were producing.

The years of neglect showed in the interior of the house as well as the gardens outside. I could only imagine how beautiful it must have been. The sunroom glass was leaking here and there, and the kitchen was very dark with old paint and poor lighting.

There was a mysterious grotto among the fir trees and large magnolias in the back of the house. As I walked to the grotto, I could smell the wonderful fragrance of the magnolias in bloom. Standing in the sunroom, I was very close to the giant white blossoms. The magnolia tree

Wilma and Leda, 1940s.

shaded the pool table area. It seemed planned that way: people could play pool and drink in the essence of the lovely, fragrant blooms.

The grotto was a rough man-made cave big enough for several people to enter. The story was that the owners of the villa, during the affluent years, had large parties. The grounds were full of surprises: hidden paths, an old stone staircase to the forest above, and large open areas in the trees where games were played. One tale told of how the host would invite guests to the grotto for wine tasting, then he would turn a secret switch that would release a fine spray of water to catch the unsuspecting.

The forest above the grotto could be reached by a long, narrow cobblestone stair that was covered with ivy and surrounded by tall pines and firs. Here and there fragrant violets and cyclamens were scattered among the trees. The villa was truly a rich playground, but not for us.

While growing up we had been accustomed to a nice home where we had marble floors and a beautiful bathroom. Now in our early teens we had to live in conditions below our previous standards. Here we had no room of our own, and we were lucky to still have a few pieces of our furniture, brought from Fiume. With my mother's care, those few pieces of furniture were still in original shape.

We had no clothes to wear to school, having grown out of all the clothes we had, and we could not buy anything new. I had to watch my mother sinking deeper and deeper into depression. I implored her and she promised to make new skirts out of other clothes, but she could not get organized to do it. I was persistent and stubborn, asking her to make clothes for us, not able to understand why she could not. She did not make her feelings known and could only retaliate by becoming angry. She used to love sewing and was proud of her Singer sewing machine, one of the items she could not part with in the move.

I had to wear the same skirt and blouse to school every day, and the other girls noticed. When I was little, I always had pretty clothes to wear, with colorful aprons to keep them clean—all made by my mother. Now I was twelve and thirteen years old and embarrassed by so many things.

In the winter in this villa we had to scrounge for firewood. The only heat we had was from an inefficient old clay stove. Sometimes it was very difficult to find wood in the snow. When spring came, my mother spent all her time in the garden, now converted to vegetables. Often I would start making soup because my mother would not come in until late at night, and we were hungry. It seemed she existed on coffee and some bread. Father was in the tuberculosis sanitarium during this time, so it was just Mother, Wilma, and me.

One summer day I talked my sister into going to the orchard of the farms on the hillside where there were fruit trees. In midday the farmers were resting, so we climbed over the fences and found ourselves in the midst of an apple and pear orchard. We started filling our gathered cotton skirts with fruit and we thought we were safe as the farmers don't start working the fields again until later in the afternoon. Instead, a red-faced *contadina* (peasant) came running and yelling after us. We went down a dry creek bed to escape, but my sister froze in fear and could not run. I had to go back and pull her until she could walk, but then she would stop again, frightened. We finally made our way back over the fence and hoped the woman didn't know who the thieves were.

Years later, when I visited Italy with my teenage sons, I walked to the edge of this farm and behold! The same *contadina* with the same red apron came out. I said: "You don't know me, but I remember you!" She smiled knowingly and said: "Yes, I do remember you and your sister. It is good to see you!"

The village of Riaglietto consisted of a small group of houses with one store; running through it was the road to Sestriere. Surrounding the village were scattered fields and farmhouses inhabited by families that had lived there for generations. When they saw us at the store, they stared as people do with strangers in their midst. In bigger towns it is not quite as noticeable. I remember going to the store to buy sugar or flour or some other item and having to ask to put the bill on the "account" because we didn't have money. I detected annoyance on the face of the storekeeper. There is no kindness when it comes to money. We always paid our small account later, when Pastor Guy would help us financially.

My father was in the tuberculosis sanitarium and helpless with his illness. There was no such a thing as public assistance then, nor any welfare agency. It was all up to us. We lived off our garden for the most part, or bartered items with farmers nearby. Mother would wash clothes in exchange and was willing to do anything, but people did not help as much, and could not understand our situation because they never had been in it themselves. They had their farms, their homes, and their families; but we had no one and hardly anything.

We lived at the villa long enough to experience two summers and one winter. My sister and I went to Pinerolo to school. At the beginning my father worked at the local foundry. We traveled every day on a train from Riaglietto to Pinerolo, a much bigger city. The hardest times were when my father could no longer work due to his tuberculosis.

Papa and Mama at Villa Vittoria.

When we first moved to the villa, my mother, as was her habit, spent hours in the garden. She salvaged some roses and peonies that had long been abandoned and completely relandscaped the garden. She cleaned the debris from the pond and restored it by adding water from the well. In fact, all our water came from the well, and the only running water was in the kitchen sink. She planted vegetables so that we always had enough to make soups and vegetable dishes. We also had rabbits and chickens.

One big white rabbit was our pet and roamed free in the garden. We also had Lilli, a cat that had at least three litters of kittens, which we could neither feed nor give away. We had a small sheltie that my father brought home after work. In those days we could take care of him, and we named him Mucchi. With father gone, we were on hard times, but our pets were very important, especially for my mother.

Mother had to do the washing in the kitchen sink, then put the clean wash in buckets and carry it to the river for rinsing. We could not use all the water from the sink. The little river that came down from the mountains to the old mill passed near the villa property. We carried the heavy buckets of washing across a trail to reach the river.

Summers were warm and beautiful. The only sadness was watching my mother working in the garden, hour after hour, forgetting about us and the meals that needed to be prepared. She was probably thinking of what life had done to her family and of the loss of her two sons. Often I saw her trying to hide tears while working with her head low in the flowers and vegetables. Maybe she knew even then that she would lose us too.

Winters were cold in this region, with lots of snow. This was ski country, and from high in the villa, I could watch the streams of cars, skis on top, headed for Sestriere. I said to myself, "Someday, I too will ski!"

Our life at Villa Vittoria ended after my father's tuberculosis was discovered and he left for the sanitarium. Nothing had been stable for us after the war, but I didn't know our life together would also end.

46 FOOD FOR THOUGHT

THIS WAS THE time that I thought we would be a normal family, with school, home, and our family reunited. But it was one of our most difficult times. I was in my early teens and my sister, two years younger, appeared oblivious to our predicament. I knew she was aware but unable to really believe it.

Today, thinking back, I can relate to my teenage years with those of today's young people. These years were difficult, as they are today. I wanted so much to blend in at school, wanted to have normal clothes, and be like other girls. Today is no different.

I was very self-conscious and also very hard on my mother, sometimes even yelling and talking badly to her. I was wearing clothes made from other clothes that my mother reconstructed on the sewing machine. I wore the same blouse and skirt every day. I could not accept the fact that we did not have any money to buy anything, even food; certainly not fabric to make clothes. We simply had no income.

And yet I wanted to blame my parents for our situation. Maybe children do this until they mature and understand better. In my case, I felt I was doing everything—helping wash clothes, then fold them, and cooking. I just wanted Mother to sew up something for me to wear to school. I expected too much; maybe she did not have enough material even when she had taken apart some other garments. This was one part of my difficult teenage transition. On the other hand, I could see how much Mother was suffering.

Sometimes when we were in the kitchen and had no visible food to prepare, I would start a soup with vegetables from our garden. Mother always had things growing in every comer of the yard. She loved to grow things, and maybe this was her only comfort then. She would be there and, lost in her helplessness, would say, "If only had flour and other ingredients, I would make so many good things for you."

My father, always the optimist (later, not in these sad times) told me a story I always remember: "There was a hobo who started to make a soup on the open fire. He started the soup with a large rock boiling in the water, pretending it was a soup bone. Others would stop by and make fun of it, but they felt bad for him even while they ridiculed him. Then one by one they started to bring an onion, then potatoes, then other food. By the end of all the cooking he had a great soup, and they all gathered around and had a good meal."

Recently I was on a trip to Europe. I realized how important food is to most people; for me it is only to nourish the body the best way possible, and then to be thankful. Talk centered much of the time around places to eat and comparing dishes of food, just discussing the meals. On this trip the dinner hour was late in the evening, lasting two to three hours with at least three courses. It was not that way for us in Villa Vittoria because we had homework and then had to get up early for school. Our dinner consisted of a single dish: polenta and tomato sauce with some meat, or just vegetables cooked with potatoes, or *capusta*—cabbage and noodles. We also had our pets, Mucchi and Lilli, to feed. For the rabbits my sister and I would go into the valley below and gather grass and clover.

My memory goes back to Fiume when Mother was cooking lots of good food and special meals for different occasions. At Easter she made the traditional sweet bread, breaded with a boiled egg in the middle. At Christmas she baked all the sweet rolls made with nuts. All our meals were very tasty, with meat and sauces; she used a lot paprika, as Hungarians do. She loved to cook and make us happy.

This is what I remember most: food was happiness because it was shared with love.

47 THE DECISION

AS WE WERE first getting settled in Villa Vittoria, we discovered that my father had contracted tuberculosis in the prison camp. He was ordered to a sanitarium in the mountains.

My Aunt Irene felt stranded in Milan. She had a job, but no particular attachment to anyone there. She had always been part of our family, and my mother wanted to make her feel that Wilma and I were like children of her own, as she had none. She visited us often in Piemonte and became even closer in discussing our future. My parents and my aunt knew that my sister and I had a poor chance of a start in life with my father unable to support us for an indefinite period. We were almost foreigners here, where families had lived for generations and shared their history together.

The three—my parents and Zia Irene—discussed all the pros and cons of young girls emigrating alone to the United States as "displaced persons." We had that political status because Fiume had become part of Yugoslavia after the war, and the majority of the citizens became *profughi* (refugees) and left the area.

This meant again separating our family and depriving our parents of their two remaining children. I know my mother and father ached at the thought of losing us. Aunt Irene helped them make the decision, "I will go with them! I will emigrate too!"

This was some consolation, at least for the moment. My mother was always strong and brave and my father was always an optimist. Their philosophy might as well have been, "Life is either a daring adventure, or nothing." So the decision was made with the firm plan that they would follow us as soon as my father was declared cured of TB.

In 1950 all our papers were in progress for my sister, me, and my aunt to emigrate. This required several months in a refugee camp in Bagnoli, near Naples. Bagnoli was a very small town where the Americans and other countries had established a processing center in the old barracks of the Italian army. We were kept busy with the bureaucratic procedures and didn't see much of anything outside the camp, but we watched with great interest the baseball games played by the American occupational forces.

The camp was very large, with hundreds of refugees, and we lost track of Aunt Irene. She was being processed in a different group, as she was an adult and considered Hungarian even though she lived all of her life in Italy. But we were confident that the three of us would all be leaving at the same time.

Wilma, age eleven. 1948.

As it turned out, Aunt Irene was not able to qualify for the United States quota and was sent instead to Toronto, Canada. We didn't know what was happening until much later, when we were already in the United States. My parents thought she would still be near us and so did we, not realizing how vast are the distances are between eastern Canada and the western United States.

Leda in Milan, 1950.

Finally, my sister and I were boarding a train for the port of Bremen, Germany. The parting was very sad. Our little family gathered at the train station in Torino. We spent a very short, difficult time together.

When my sister and I were on board and the train started moving, they walked slowly alongside the train, then as fast as they could. Then my father slowed, trying to prevent some agony, but my mother kept going. Finally I saw her faltering and reaching for a bench. She sat down, my father near her, she leaning her head on his shoulder while he put his arms around her. Both pressed their white hankies to their eyes, their heads no longer holding up with courage.

As the train pulled away, my sister and I leaned out the window, waving farewell, "*Arrivederci!*" until I could only see my parents as two tiny dots on the platform. Then there was only silence and many tears; my mother's heart was broken, all her children taken away from her.

48 Un Sogno (A Dream)

"*LA VITA É un sogno sfuggente* (Life is a fleeting dream)," my mother wrote in my remembrance book, adding to my schoolmates' parting words at the end of the school year. She said this to me other times; she meant that life can slip away quickly, like a dream, and in the morning be gone. The last seven years of her life were sad and difficult. My sister and I, her only remaining children, were gone from her life—like a dream.

So often I had heard my mother singing in the happy years, and also in the sad years later, songs from the operas. She would sing: "*Un bel dí*" from *Madama Butterfly* and arias from *Traviata*, *La Bohème*, and *La Forza del Destino*. I had a feeling that she sang to reflect her life. After the war, I heard more haunting and sad songs, as if she were waiting in vain like Cio-Cio-San.

My mother had a premonition of sorrowful times ahead that turned out to be true. In 1948–49, shortly after our family was reunited, it became evident that our life was not going well. We had left Fiume, our hometown, which was overtaken by Tito's Yugoslavia, and had come to a little village near Turin. Our faithful pastor found a job for my father and housing for us through friends.

Before the war, my father was a specialized foundry worker in the shipyard; he was one of builders of the twin ships *Saturnia* and *Vulcania*. Now he started working in a foundry again, commuting to his job early in the morning and coming home late at night. He was always cheerful and happy to have a job. The old villa where we lived was lovely in many ways, but the steep walk up to it left him short of breath. He was exhausted when he came home and started coughing more and more.

A doctor's examination revealed tuberculosis, probably acquired in the concentration camp.

Even in this state he continued his habitual optimism, writing in my memory book: "*La vita comincia domani* (Life begins tomorrow)," by which he meant, "There is always a tomorrow." While he was comforting, my mother had a sense of quiet prophecy, and she was always right, I knew. Maybe time does not mean anything. We only realize this just when time is almost gone. A lifetime may really be just an instant. When a person is dying, it has been reported, they see their whole lifetime in a brief moment.

Of course, we all had to commute from the village of Riaglietto to the more distant city of Pinerolo, to school or bigger stores or even a movie. This is where I remember going to my first movie with my mother, probably to escape the world of sadness that now was with her all the time. We saw *The Adventures of Baron Munchausen*, and *The Thief of Bagdad*. I will always remember them.

We were happy to have a home, and I remember well the series of terraces on top of the garage and gardener quarters. The cement was cracked in many places, showing the years of neglect. We rested here after the long hill and before tackling the second little hill to the house. I loved the view of the vineyards and the valley below. I visualized potted geraniums on the balconies, absent now with the villa abandoned.

Our parents wanted us to have an education or a trade so we could always have a job. Now that was impossible, with my father unable to work. After elementary schools (free in Italy), there were only tuition schools, and there was no money for that. We took a few trips in the mountains to visit Father in the sanitarium, and Mother and Father would walk and talk together while my sister and I went to pick flowers in the hills.

We had the option to emigrate to any of the three countries—the United States, New Zealand, Australia—but with my father's condition, we could not go as a family. Our parents made the supreme sacrifice: to let their daughters emigrate to the United States, giving us a chance to go to school and have a better life. Our life together was coming to an end.

My mother sang the songs of doom, like Butterfly giving up her child. She had always given her whole self to the family; now everything had to be given up, and her future was inescapable sadness.

Our last weeks in old Villa Vittoria were days of silent desperation, where my mother spoke very little to avoid crying in front of us. She hid her face from us by working in the garden for long hours, never looking up. I knew her tears were falling on the ground where she was working. *Grandi dolori sono muti* (Big pain is mute). Mother was lost in a world of deep sadness, even forgetting to make meals.

She had only lived for her children and the family, and now everything had to be given up. She lived with her songs that kept her breathing a little longer. Her silence would only escape in her singing all the arias she knew so well. She sang with all her heart in the kitchen, and I could hear her upstairs and outside in the garden. Her beautiful voice floated in the air and embraced me wherever I was—while I studied for exams or took care of chores.

My father's philosophy sustained her. He never gave up hope and tried to be cheerful, while Mother was unable to accept our parting and think of a possible reunion later. She seemed to know in her heart that she would never see us again.

At the sanitarium my father had to have a lung surgery, and Mother remained alone for two years. She would limp down and up the steep hill to the village to get the mail.

After we left, the dream of reuniting with us kept her alive for seven years, but then her heart gave out. Father's did the same, but ten years later at almost the same time of year. He was able to emigrate shortly after my mother died. He shared his life with my sister and me for those ten years. His words are still with me, "Laugh. Life is short, don't be mad."

He was right. There is always a new day. "Life begins again tomorrow!"

49 Arrivederci, Italia

NEAR NAPLES WAS a large refugee center where Americans and other countries like Australia and New Zealand were processing papers for immigration. My sister and I were involved with the American offices.

We had one interview where they asked us: "How come you are going without your parents? How do you feel about this? Can you part

Leda, age fifteen, 1951.

with your parents?" and many other questions. They already knew our background; they were testing us. I remember having to explain that we were just like orphans because our parents could not take care of us and were both sick. This is how we entered the world of children without family, and they gave us a button that said, "U.S. CHILD."

We were in the Naples camp for about a month while our papers were being processed. My Aunt Irene was in another part of the camp getting her papers processed for Canada. She was very busy during this time and we did not see her. The fact that we did not get to emigrate together was a great regret in her life, but she felt this was for the best as she did not want to interfere with our placement. We needed a placement in a family, and she needed work to get settled as an individual.

From Naples we traveled across Italy into the Alps, and arrived in Bremen in a couple of days. I have very little recollection of this trip, perhaps because of the shock of leaving our parents and the trauma of the separation. The train stopped in Bolzano, and our cousin Nini (Aunt Emilia's son), now a young man who lived in this city, made an effort to be there to see us for a moment while the train stopped. We only saw a glimpse of him as he was trying to get to the train on his bike. We only saw him enough to wave goodbye.

I can see now how children can be traumatized by a separation from their parents and then retain this fear later in life. At different times I have found it very difficult to part with anyone or anything that has played a significant role in my life.

We were in Bremen a short period of time, a few weeks. Here we were in a large army camp, probably used by the Germans during the war, now converted to a refugee camp. I remember walking to a large plaza in the camp where a lot of the refugees gathered. My sister and I and an Italian girl stayed together for moral support. We were surrounded by people speaking numerous languages. There were no other Italians and no one who even spoke Italian.

Finally we boarded a navy ship for the transatlantic voyage. The ship was small, and we had bunk beds three or four high. The mess hall was small and cramped, and I can still smell it—a special type of smell.

During the trip on the ocean we had many days of very rough seas. The ship would ride up on a big wave and then plunge down. It was scary, and I was often seasick. Sometimes, to prevent the sickness, my sister and I would go on deck to the fresh air and sing at the top of our voices. Nobody could hear us with the roar of the sea. The singing seemed to help the waves of nausea and vomiting, most probably because we concentrated on something other than our stomachs. It kept our minds off the fear, too.

During meals I was kept very busy helping with the small children and setting tables. My sister, being younger, was not required to work. All the time aboard, I really doubted we would ever reach land. I was sure that one of the times the ship went down into a hole in the sea, it would not come back up.

When we finally sailed into New York Harbor, we marveled at the Statue of Liberty. New York appeared to be a magical city of lights. It was like a dream; we never had seen a city this big. We went through Ellis Island with the usual waiting and paperwork processing. We were all lined up to go through offices, accompanied by adults who could speak for us.

Mama and Papa, 1950.

We finally arrived at the Youth Center. I always felt so grateful to the people helping us; they smiled and talked to us in a soft voice. I felt welcomed. I knew that real love and kindness was present in all the people that met us at the port and then took us to the center, which was in the Bronx.

I made the trip from Naples to Bremen and then New York in a kind of trance, performing all that was asked of me like a robot. Once in the Youth Center, I felt safe. Responding to the love the people were showing us, I finally came alive again. Now I could feel inside me the warmth of people and the caring they showed. I could live now and maybe become normal. I was not afraid anymore.

I knew then as now that American people are incredibly generous and willing to help the unfortunate. A few years ago, as an American couple was traveling through southern Italy with their child, the boy was killed by bandits in an ambush. Despite their grief, the parents donated a part of the body—something unheard of in Italy. I'm sure since that time Italians learned something different than they ever knew—happiness comes from working for the happiness of others.

One of the songs we sang on the ship was this:

Sta sera gli angeli non volano,
ma piangono per noi.
Piangono perché te ne vai.

Sta sera gli alberi si abbracciano
perché vogliono nasconderci dalla luna,
amica del nostro amore.

Non dirmi che tornerai
perché non lo farai,
lo so non ti vedrò,
non ti vedrò mai più.

Tra poco tu te ne andrai,
io so che piangerò
ma poi mi scorderò,
mi scorderò di te.

Sta sera gi angeli non volano,
ma piangono per noi,
piangono per me e per te.

The English translation:

The angels do not fly tonight,
but they cry for us.
They cry because you're leaving.

The trees embrace each other
because they want to hide us from the moon,
friend of our love.

Do not tell me you'll come back
because you will not do it,
I know I will not see you,
I'll never see you again.

Soon you will leave,
I know that I will cry,
but then I will forget
I will forget you.

The angels do not fly tonight,
but they cry for us,
they cry for me and for you.

How appropriate for our fate, as we never saw our mother again, our dearest love.

50 THE CENTER

IN NEW YORK City the World Council of Churches had a refugee children's center that was either a gift or a loan from somebody rich. The three-story structure must have been a grand old residence at one time. It had many rooms and a stairway to the front entrance. I vaguely remember our three-month stay there in the fall of 1950, and I only remember the first and second floors.

The first floor had a broad entrance adjacent to a large room. This was our main area, with many tables and chairs. There was a kitchen and dining room on this floor. I can't remember any meals in particular, but everything was wonderful though different from food I had at home in Italy—Jell-O, for example, was completely new to me. The bedrooms were on the second floor.

What I remember most are the children of all ages—from very small toddlers to teenagers. Since my sister and I were teenagers, we mostly associated with our own age group.

Of the twenty to thirty children living there at that time, there were only about ten our age, and only one other Italian girl about the same age. This girl, however, was going to some member of her family in New York City. She was the only one who had some place to go. She had made the trip with us to Bremen, and then to New York in the U.S. Navy ship.

My biggest regret has been that we did not keep in touch with these children. We were all waiting day by day to hear where we would be going. We didn't even know the address until we arrived at our destination, and we were all going to different parts of the country. I didn't even know when anybody was leaving—suddenly they were just gone.

These fellow refugee children were the ones we would have had so much in common with in our new lives, and we could have been some support to each other if we had been able to stay in touch. Life was flying by fast; I'm sure we all had a lot of adjusting to do and many problems to deal with.

Kicci (not sure of correct spelling) was a Hungarian boy of about fifteen. He arrived at the center before us, and he tried to be extra nice to newcomers. He would sit by us at the table, showing love by smiling and helping in every way. He was what we call an "old soul." He had compassion for us, for the loss of our parents, and he tried to be a brother to us. Not knowing our language, he couldn't speak to us, but his expressions were loving and showed willingness to help.

Kicci was stocky and must have worked hard in his short life. Even his hands were those of a worker, not of a young boy. His Hungarian features—olive skin, dark eyes, and easy, warm smile—reminded me of my mother. I told him that my mother was from Budapest and then he became especially close to us.

He accompanied us to the baseball games nearby—this was our introduction to baseball. I didn't understand anything about it, but almost all the older children went as a group to the games, and Kicci would always sit by us.

Another special boy was Gusty. He was Jewish and very small for his age of fourteen or fifteen. Still, his face was old. He seemed out of place somehow, and I'm not sure what language he spoke. Words were not important at this point; I understood so much more from their actions and expressions. There were certainly more boys than girls in the older group.

It seemed to me that almost every child spoke a different language, but sometimes I could see two speaking to each other. The languages were Russian, Czech, German, Hungarian, and others I could not identify—maybe Latvian and Finnish. We did not understand each other at all, and as far as I could tell, nobody spoke English.

We were divided into different classes around the house—in different rooms or corners—to learn English. My sister and I must have been the worst at English because "Mr. Jim" decided to give us extra tutoring. One important first sentence that we had to learn, according to Mr. Jim, was "I don't know."

One day when we were walking around the streets, someone asked us something. Of course, we didn't understand a word and so we said, "I don't know." The man looked very disgruntled while he kept on walking and pointing to his wrist. He had not pointed to his wrist when he first spoke, and we certainly were very quick with our new sentence. Apparently, he wanted to know the time.

We had a lot of free time, which we spent roaming the city and taking all the subways. We always went in groups, accompanied by the more experienced kids who had been at the refugee center for a while and knew the city. We lived somewhere in the Bronx, and we became very good at finding all the other areas in New York City by subway.

Mr. Jim led us to his beautiful apartment to show us how to get there for our lessons. Sometimes he would turn the TV on. It was the first time we ever saw a television. He told us to listen carefully, and our eyes were glued to the screen. Now and then he would ask, "Did we understand some words?" No, we didn't understand anything. Mr. Jim was the most outstanding character in my life then, and even now. I think of him as an amazing, unusually gifted man.

Mr. Jim was tall with blond, curly hair; a very good-looking man, perhaps in his forties, although I was not then a good judge of age. Now, as I think back, he may have been in his fifties. He was very thin and distinguished-looking, with perfect, well-proportioned features and blue eyes—always impeccably and tastefully dressed. He moved with grace and agility, and to me he appeared aristocratic.

The amazing thing about Mr. Jim was that he could speak so many languages so perfectly. He spoke Italian so well that I was convinced he was born in Italy, somewhere in the northern part where there are many tall, blond people. He was a teaser, and would even talk to us in some Italian dialect that only a native could have spoken. And he led us to believe that he was Italian, always smiling when he said so.

One day I managed to communicate with Kicci. "Did Mr. Jim speak Hungarian well?" It is well-known that Hungarian is a difficult language to master. Kicci nodded, smiling. "Yes, yes, he Hungarian." I knew that this could not be so because he spoke Italian too perfectly. Then I questioned the Russians and the Latvians, and the answer was the same: he was Russian, or he was Latvian.

On a day when Mr. Jim was giving us our private English lessons, I started to investigate with persistent questions. Finally he said, "I am really English, from Britain, but I traveled all over the world." It was amazing to me that he could speak so many languages so well that native speakers could not detect an accent. I have never known a person like Mr. Jim in all the years since. He spoke all the languages, including Russian and Greek.

Our stay in New York City was short but memorable. One by one, all of the children were placed in different homes. Our little group of two Italians, two or three Czechs, two Russians, a Hungarian, and a Latvian stayed close. I cannot remember many of the names because they were strange to me at the time, being used to only Italian names. I really believe there might have been a deliberate effort for us not to bond too closely, however, as our lives would go in all different directions and we saw parting as very sad. This was the fall of 1950.

When we become older there is a stronger desire to have close friends. So many times in later years I longed to see and talk to the "kids" of the refugee center. I missed Mr. Jim so much, and yet I did not attempt or know how to get in touch with him when he was still there. We loved Mr. Jim, and we understood that he was very special. He was generous with himself—a real "giver." I believe he was working for a good cause, where he spent all his days with refugee children rather than at a prestigious job. He had a special talent with languages, and he shared this gift in a very unselfish way. I don't believe he was working for money.

When I volunteered at the international Goodwill Games in the Northwest (Tacoma and Seattle) in the 1980s, I saw a difference. I was a translator for the Italian pentathlon team. Some athletes asked me how much I was earning at this job. They were totally surprised by my answer, that I was a volunteer—unheard of in Italy by a majority of people, I suspect. They said, "No one in Italy would do this for no pay!"

We refugees came to a rich and powerful country, and we were proud to be part of it; but most of all we came to a generous nation, willing to help the unfortunate. America was indeed rich in spirit and willing to welcome the displaced children of World War II and encourage them to make a good life.

It was a privilege to go to Mr. Jim's apartment for lessons. His home was spacious, overlooking Central Park. Many times we walked there with him as he attempted to educate us in the American way of life, a place where families and all kinds of people walked. He would take his two white Afghan dogs. As far as I knew, he lived alone with his dogs.

Still, as much as we were well taken care of, my main dread was that of the unknown. Where was everybody going? It was hard to see children leave; but when the time came, they were excited, and so we were happy for them. They were going to a home where they would be accepted. My sister and I were among the last to leave. They asked us, would we separate? But we had promised our mother that we would stay together no matter what.

The older boys we were able to understand said that they were going to states like Iowa and Nebraska, probably to be with farm families. The children were all scattered in different states where there were families willing to take them in.

This time of my life, too, had to pass, and it is almost forgotten. But the memories come back easily. I remember the perfect uniqueness of each personality. But all the faces pass by—life rushes on like a river, and we are carried in the current.

51 NEW YORK CITY

DURING THE THREE months we were at the Center, the group that had banded together dwindled to just a few of us as foster families claimed one after another. There was a sadness in this because even though our communication with each other was limited, we all shared the bond of circumstances. We were all without families of our own and we shared the apprehension of the unknown future. We knew we would never see each other again.

The other Italian girl moved on quickly because of the distant relations she had right there in the city. The rumor was that although she was only sixteen, a marriage had been arranged, but I doubted it. Our sponsor, the World Council of Churches, would never have allowed the arrangement.

The people who were working with us were all very wonderful and dedicated to our welfare. They understood our position. Mr. Jim was one of these people, and there was also a doctor who came to the center to give physical exams. We had a structured school schedule to teach us basic English. Some of us had never heard English spoken at all. Mr. Jim concentrated on these children.

The only link we had with the city of New York was Mr. Jim. He spoke all the languages, even Polish and Greek, and he could explain to all the different children in their own language. The kids were always asking questions and he would answer each one, jumping from one language to the next very easily.

We all loved Mr. Jim, and loved walking in the park with him after we had studied and practiced the language. When we were there it was study time and we could only glimpse the view from his apartment and the short period of television to see if we understood.

52 THE ARRIVAL

MY SISTER AND I were finally told that a placement had been found in Washington state. People and workers at the refugee center were saying, "Poor kids." We understood they did not consider this to be a lucky placement. Mr. Jim explained to us that Washington was very far away and had lots of snow and cold weather. Some people even believed it was still Indian country, with little wars. There were very few little children left at the center. Everyone in our age group was gone.

We found ourselves on a train. Our journey lasted at least three days and nights. I don't remember any details of eating or sleeping, but I do remember the scenery. I was glued to the windows, taking in all I could of this new land. It was all so astonishing to me, even the large prairies as we went across flat lands. Then we came to the mountain country, and I was amazed to see the snowy, alpine landscape so near the train. I had never seen anything like this, even in the little train in Pinerolo, Italy, where we had snow, but it was never so high so close to towns and cities.

When we finally arrived in Seattle, the train station looked exciting. I was anxiously looking from the windows for the two ladies who were to meet us and take us to their home. When we stepped down, there were indeed two nice ladies who very excitedly began hugging and talking to us.

Even now, after about three months of English lessons, we could not understand anything and could speak even less, but we felt we had come to caring and warm people and to the end of our journey, for now. The two sisters were even trying to talk to us in Italian, and had spent time learning enough to be able to communicate with us. These two ladies were sisters—June Nordquist and Winifred Dove.

From the train station in Seattle we headed for the downtown ferry terminal, which would take us across Puget Sound to Bremerton. This was another new experience—getting in a car and then onto a ferry with many other cars. June and Winifred were watching us all the time to see our reactions. We were overwhelmed with so many new things. I found Winifred very serious and rigid while she drove a big Nash, in comparison to people in Italy who drove little cars with seemingly little effort. I used to watch cars whizzing by in Riaglietto on their way to the ski slopes at Sestriere. Here, everything was so orderly—getting onto the ferry and driving so slowly and carefully.

In Bremerton, we arrived at a street that was lined with a row of brick houses. This was different from Italy, where housing was usually in large buildings at least two stories high. It was different from Florence, where the apartment buildings were really large; or Pinerolo in an isolated mountain villa; or in Fiume, where our home was in duplex row housing with many dwellings.

This Bremerton neighborhood had blocks of separate houses where people were seldom seen in the streets. They were just getting into their car in the garage and coming or going. Of course, we arrived in wintertime. People seemed really isolated from their neighbors. At the same time, we almost thought the sisters' house was a little villa, with a very small garden and pond in the back.

We felt very lucky.

53 JUNE AND WINIFRED

TWO WONDERFUL LADIES offered to take in two "orphan" girls from another country. Looking back, I can see what a great, unselfish thing they did, what an enormous challenge they took on.

What I remember and could understand at the time was that they themselves were orphans at a young age, while my sister and I at least still had our parents in Italy, though they were unable to provide for us. Father was in a tuberculosis sanatorium and Mother was suffering from poor physical health and mental depression resulting from the difficult war years.

June and Winifred were from Havre, Montana, where their mother died early in their childhood and their father was a traveling worker in the popular circuses of that time. The sisters were taken in by some kind relatives, but eventually they had to make their own way in life. June married, but Winifred, who was very involved with the church, never married. She worked with Native Americans in the West. June became a teacher while Winifred continued to work in the Pueblo villages of Colorado.

June married a Swedish immigrant named Roy Nordquist. They eventually settled in Bremerton, Washington, where June's husband worked in the naval shipyard. Many members of the Nordquist family moved to this area, and Roy and his brothers helped each other build cabins on Hood Canal that still remain in the family. When Roy died, the couple had two grown children. June asked her sister to come live with her in Bremerton. They both worked as teachers at Bremerton High School.

These two women assumed responsibility for my sister and me when we came into their home at ages 13 and 15 with no understanding of the

English language or American customs, from a war-torn country and a family whose background they knew nothing of.

I didn't realize at the time how much they did for us. In addition to giving us a home, they helped us gain American citizenship and requested the assistance of government officials to help our parents also immigrate to the United States. All the while, they worked at demanding jobs as teachers and helped Wilma and me understand a language and culture that were new to us. It was difficult for me especially, but they were very patient and worked with us as much as possible, at the same time maintaining relationships with their own family members.

They will always be in my memory—these two wonderful women who gave their all to two young immigrant girls. There are not enough words to express my appreciation of June and Winifred.

54 SUDDENLY, NO FAMILY

MY SISTER AND I, coming to this country with no family, had just gone through a deep shock, and we were only barely able to realize the extent of this fact. Although we managed to conceal our feelings of isolation by being involved in an entirely different life than we had ever known, we felt totally alone in the midst of strangers and totally dependent on the two kind, elderly teachers who had given us a home. We were refugee children of World War II.

In our early years, we had a close, nurturing family, but now my sister and I had no one but each other. We were foreigners, with different customs and background. June and Winifred tried to understand us, as we in turn tried to understand them and our new life.

Everybody we came across at school, church and elsewhere, had some aunts, cousins, grandparents, etc.—but not us. We were so busy with life, school, and the language barrier, yet we could only partly take our minds away from our situation. Three months of English lessons in the New York City refugee children's center was not enough to learn the language. Foreign language lessons were offered in schools in Italy, and I had taken French—the only choice in my grade.

It must have been inconceivable to the teenagers in school or church: two girls coming from another country and alone. In 1951, not many foreigners lived there, at least not in Bremerton.

As soon as we arrived in January 1951, we enrolled at Bremerton High School, taking classes in math, English, choir, typing, gym, and home economics . . . and we did not understand much of anything. We could understand math and typing, but following recipes and measuring was a struggle. I had to ask for help from the teachers every step of the way.

As June and Winifred were devout Methodists, we immediately were introduced to their church's Methodist Youth Fellowship (MYF). It turned out to be a good experience and a place where we made life-long friends. We were busy, but we still had no family. We came from nowhere, as far as the people there understood. In those days people did not travel much, and Italy was a faraway country. Some people in New York didn't even know where Washington state was, or they said that it was on the other side of the "world," where people were still almost pioneers a country full of Indians.

We had such a wonderful family, and no one will know unless I write about it. We were not just two people coming here from nowhere, a far-away country. We were products of life and fate. Like a swift river, life takes us to our destiny. The current will not stop; it will only go around the obstacles. The intuition of my parents was correct. We found a new home, and we adjusted after many years. Their spirit is with us always, giving us courage and strength. "Life begins tomorrow."

55 New Beginnings

LIFE WITH JUNE and Winifred was certainly different from our previous experience. Now there were schedules and rules. We were expected to eat at certain exact times, and all our activities were supervised. I felt controlled and not free anymore. In Italy, with my family, I was free to use my judgment and make decisions. There were no certain times to eat or go to bed. In other words, no one would tell us it was time to go to sleep or time to do our homework. We knew what had to be done: eat what was available for dinner, study or we would not pass our tests, go to bed so we could get up early to catch the little train to school in town.

We had a good upbringing when we were little, and now we were entering teenage years and becoming responsible for our actions. In Pinerolo there were a lot of times after school when I had to cook some soups and some dinners. I knew what we had to do. Mother was coping with life as best as she could.

We lived now in a modest brick house, not far from the high school. June and Winifred were very active in the Methodist Church, which was part of the World Council of Churches, I presumed. This is why they committed to the responsibility of taking in two teenage girls from a foreign country who were complete strangers. They felt safer to have some rules and routines by which to live with us there. They had the same rules with their own children and in school as teachers. June had a grown son and daughter, while Winifred was well-disciplined as a deaconess earlier in life.

Even in New York City we were free to roam the streets and subways all by ourselves. The people working in the refugee center were tolerant, trusting, and knowledgeable of children's needs and behavior from so many different walks of life. Of course, New York City in the 1950s was safer than it is now.

In Italy I learned to cook just from observing my mother in the kitchen—certainly not from recipes—and only with ingredients available. Here we were being taught cooking from a book, with measurements I had never heard of.

In Italy I improvised soups using ingredients from our vegetable garden. I helped my mother in every way I could think of as I saw her becoming more and more distraught. I knew she was thinking all the time that our life was not turning out well.

In our new home, everything was highly regulated. Winifred was especially strict about what time to come for breakfast and what time to leave the house for school, and she expressed herself very firmly. I found it difficult to live in such a regimented way. While before I was my own boss, now I could not be five minutes late for breakfast.

On the other hand, June and Winifred were very patient and forgiving with us. Once they scolded us very seriously because we went with some of the church group to watch Elvis Presley on TV at somebody's house. We did not call to let them know what we were doing. After all, this was a new way of life—reporting all our actions. They tried to make us understand some of these rules. We did not grow up with rules of this sort. At times we were felt hurt, and Winifred especially talked to us and counseled us. We were always forgiven.

At Bremerton High School, June was in charge of the history and social studies classes while Winifred taught mathematics and photography. School was fine, even if I felt like a "fish out of water." There were stares as other kids studied us—our every move, how we walked, and how we acted. They had never seen a person from another country before.

Today I know that in Italy people watch Americans, British, or other visitors, and they often have a preconceived idea of each personality. They love Americans for their easy smiles and have their own ideas about other foreigners. But back then, in Bremerton, I thought Wilma and I were the only ones in that situation where we were under observation.

One time, during a school assembly (a totally new concept for us), my sister and I were invited to come to the stage and talk about our background. We were asked, "What do you think of the clothes here?" and many other questions. I could hardly understand and answer but managed somehow.

I said, "The saddle shoes look like boys' shoes and are not very attractive." Everybody laughed. I don't remember what else was asked, but the whole time there was a lot of laughter after every answer, which was in very poor English, I'm sure. None of it was very funny to me, and I hated to be in the limelight.

Mr. Manzo, the choir director, looked like a typical Italian, but he was not especially helpful or warm to us, keeping us at a distance that I interpreted as "swim or drown." His primary job was to direct a choir, which he did with style and much facial expression. He had a special relationship with sopranos and the pupils whose good voices he could always depend on.

At home we were tutored by June and Winifred, who were armed with an Italian dictionary. They had traveled in Europe and wanted to learn Italian. It was not a bad idea: we needed to learn English and they, Italian. But they sacrificed their wish so that we could learn English. They wanted us to learn English as quickly as possible, so Italian became a secondary language. They were firm that we now would have to talk to each other only in English, which we did. It seemed so strange and yet funny. We got used to it, and to this day we don't speak to each other in Italian.

There was one bright spot in my two years of high school: the other kids were mostly nice to us. A boy named Ron would walk to school with us and also wait after classes to walk us home (his home was nearby). A girl named Charlotte would wait for us in the morning outside the door to walk with us to school, as June and Winifred had to leave earlier in the morning for their classes. We joined the MYF and formed lasting friendships there. To this day, we still have some close friends from our high school days.

One American practice that was completely new to us was the concept of an "allowance." We could not grasp it at first but eventually understood that we were supposed to use it to buy new clothes for school. Instead, all of our allowance money went straight to our mother in Italy. While Father was in the hospital, she had no income. These were hard times for our parents, and they needed the money a lot more than I needed new clothes.

I didn't see anything wrong with wearing the same clothes for several days, because I did not get dirty. The other students did wear different clothes almost every day, which was strange to me.

After graduation, everybody went in different directions, but we kept in touch with some of the friends we made in those years. They knew us when we didn't even speak English. Throughout the years we've tried to take at least one hiking trip in the summer, as we did with the high school climbing club.

These first years of our separation were very hard for our parents. I'm sure they spent most of their time talking about us and waiting for our letters. While we were immersed in a new life, our parents suffered, living only for our not-too-frequent correspondence; the money we sent was an assurance that we were doing well. I could feel my parents' suffering from their own writing, and sometimes, I'm sure, there were dried tears in those letters they sent.

56 La Forza del Destino (The Force of Destiny)

MOTHER OFTEN SAID, "I will never be a burden to you," and she meant she would never be a weight—either sick or dependent on us. She wanted us to be free. I believe that is why she decided on the surgery—because she felt there was no further purpose in her life and knew what the end result would be.

Mama, 1955.

Our letters from America were not frequent, and our lives were busy. Mother understood. She knew we were free and that we had opened up our wings and flown from her nest. Her heart was not well, her legs were not well, and she had experienced lower abdominal pain over the past few years. I heard it was appendicitis but not acute.

Wilma and I were getting closer to being able to have our parents join us here in the United States. We had been in the country seven years, and we both had jobs and contact with people who could help us make arrangements for Mother and Father's immigration. I had lived with this one thought in my mind, to reunite with our parents. Their sacrifice and unselfishness were now to be repaid.

Without mentioning it in one of their letters, Mother went into the hospital to have the abdominal surgery she needed. She did not want us to be preoccupied with her; she wanted us to take care of our own lives and not worry about her. My dear mother had risked her life during the war. She had always been the constant nurturer, the unselfish one, and she believed in her children to her last breath. Still, she worried about being a "weight" on us here.

One day June and Winifred approached us hesitantly, asking us to sit down so that we could talk. They had received a letter from my father asking them to break some bad news to us, gently. Before they said a word, I cried, "Mama!" My mother had died! Suddenly I had lost my most precious being, my mother, and a great part of myself as well. The emptiness I felt, the desolation and loneliness, was indescribable.

My father later wrote some details of what happened. Mother had decided to go ahead with the abdominal surgery, assuring Father that it needed to be done before coming here. At the hospital in Torino all went well—a simple appendectomy without complications.

In the evening two days following surgery, my father went home. After dinner Mother was in the recovery ward singing popular songs to the whole room. She sang so lovingly that everyone was moved to tears. They all knew her story, her dream of reuniting with her daughters.

Suddenly, while singing, she put her hand to her throat and could not breathe. She died instantly of a blood clot in her heart. Blood thinners were not available in 1957 as they are today.

Mother was sixty-one. Her life was like a dream, vanished in an instant. As she said many times to me, "*E destino.*" It was predestined, there is nothing to be done, the plan is already there.

My father was later able to reunite with us here in the United States and share ten years of his life with us. His optimism carried me through and gave me this gift: "There is another day."

57 REPRESENTATIVE PELLY

FIVE YEARS AFTER our arrival in the United States, my sister and I became citizens. We had learned sufficient English to graduate from high school and take the tests at the Immigration and Naturalization Service (INS). We had studied American history, which was completely new to us. Earlier we had studied only European history, ancient and recent, but never any American history. We were sworn in at a ceremony at the Immigration Office in Seattle in 1955.

At this point we began to give serious thought to arranging for our parents' immigration. When we broached the subject with June and Winifred, they were taken aback and surprised at our determination. They had just asked us if we wanted to be adopted by them and change our names. I found this suggestion very shocking because our parents were still alive and we were proud of our family name. We appreciated the help the two schoolteachers had given us, and we tried to repay them by doing housework and yard chores, but no one could replace our parents.

Caught off guard and incredulous at our intentions, they nonetheless went to their wise and knowledgeable friend, Romaine Nicholson. She was an interesting professor who seemed to know everything, especially about politics. She helped us in our quest by contacting Representative Thomas M. Pelly, who represented the Bremerton area in Congress at that time. We sent letters to Representative Pelly, and he was kind enough to help us with the immigration paperwork. He explained the steps we needed to take: secure a job for my father and procure sponsorship. A sponsor, as explained to us, meant someone to guarantee our parents' stay in the United States.

I was already working at Zellerback Paper Company and living independently in a small apartment in Seattle. I thought this was sufficient

Romaine Nicholson, Winifred Dove, and June Nordquist (left to right) meet in Olympia with Representative Thomas Pelly (right) in 1956 about bringing Leda's parents to the United States.

guarantee that I would take care of them. I never thought they would live anywhere else except with me.

The next step was to have a job lined up for my father. I decided to go to an "Italian company" with this request. I went to Mission Macaroni, located in south Seattle, a company I passed on my way to work. One day I just walked into the office and requested to see the person in charge. I presented my problem to the head of this company as best as I could. This kindly man listened to me attentively with a soft smile. On the strength of my words, he signed the paper giving assurance of a job in his company. I now had a work permit for my father.

I went to June and Winifred and asked them to sign the sponsorship paper. They hesitated, and were even suspicious, and did not sign right away. Eventually they agreed to sign the paper, after my insistence that I would always be responsible for my parents.

The health status of my father was cleared after his stay at the sanitarium. All these steps were certainly not easy, even with the assistance of Representative Pelly, but he was a great help in speeding up the process. Even so, it took almost a year.

It was too late for my mother. She died in 1957, just a few months before the process was completed. I never again saw the deep, sad eyes, worn out by so many tears. I would never again feel her kiss on my forehead. But her courage would be with me forever, and so I worked even harder to save my father, who remained alone and lost. He came that year by ship to New York.

At this time, my sister Wilma also started working, having finishing two years at Olympic College. We were living in a small apartment in Queen Anne when Father came to the United States. Then Wilma, through some people at her workplace, was able to find another home for us. The owner of a small building on Rainier Avenue in Seattle gave us a fairly large apartment with free utilities, in exchange for my father's work as manager of the boiler room in the basement, which supplied heat for the whole building. There were five or six apartments above small businesses and a bank. He was so happy that he could finally help us.

Thus began our life together, and we lived like we always had, everyone working for the good of our little family. Father, totally dedicated to us (even cooking meals for us), made our life so much easier.

58 REUNITED

MY FATHER SPENT his days at the hospital in Turin where Mother had abdominal surgery. The trip there was on a train for over one or two hours, depending on the connections, from Abbadia Alpina, Pinerolo, and Torino—just one way. He would come back late at night, all alone in the dark, to the old villa.

Two or three days after surgery, a small blood clot came loose, lodged in her heart, and she was gone. My father was devastated when he found

Papa, 1954.

out. There were no telephones anywhere near our home, and it was morning before someone was able to walk up the hill with the news. He had no family left and not many people who knew him in this new home. They told him to bring some clothes for burial. I remember my mother had prepared a very nice black dress, folded in a trunk, and had told me, "This will be ready when I die." She thought to take even this burden from us.

A few days later, his brother-in-law Giovanni, the husband of my mother's sister Elena, came from near Venice to help. Father had to dispose of the furniture and all of the household things he and Mother had accumulated throughout their married life. Father saved some significant items for us, which he later brought with him in a steamer trunk. Our mahogany furniture and the beloved Singer sewing machine had to be given away. The two men worked silently together at all there was to do, including the funeral.

Father's future was unknown, and only the hope of reuniting with his daughters sustained him. He could not live alone in the sad old villa, so far away from everything. After the funeral, Father went to live with Aunt Elena and Uncle Giovanni near Venice. His own family, two sisters and a niece and nephew in Yugoslavia, were unable to come for support.

On the outskirts of Venice, in the town of Mestre, he tried his best not to be of any trouble to the small family—Aunt Elena, her husband Giovanni, and Franco, their only child. He shared with them the very small pension he had. Elena's health was not good, and this may have contributed to her not being hospitable and kind. Father would spend entire days roaming the streets of Venice. This did not suit Elena, and she accused him of spending time in an *osteria*, or pub, but I know that my father never had more than a glass or two of wine with meals his whole life.

Some distant relations and good friends of Mother's throughout the years finally came to his rescue, inviting him to stay in their home in Palermo. These people, not even close relatives, were kind to him and convinced him that this was the best place to await papers for his departure to the United States.